See You On Down the Road

Also by Leon Hale

Fiction
Bonney's Place
Addison

Non-fiction
Turn South at the Second Bridge
A Smile from Katie Hattan
Easy Going
One Man's Christmas
Texas Chronicles
Home Spun
Old Friends

Memoir
Paper Hero
Supper Time

See You On Down the Road

A Retirement Journal

LEON HALE

WINEDALE PUBLISHING
Houston / Winedale

Library of Congress Cataloging-in-Publication Data
Hale, Leon, 1921-
See You on Down the Road : A Retirement Journal / Leon Hale
p. cm
ISBN 978-0-9752727-1-8 (alk. Paper)
I. Title
www.winedalebooks.com

Manufactured in the United States of America

2 4 6 8 9 7 5 3

To B.F.H., for all the reasons only she will ever know

Contents

Foreword xi

Introduction 1

2014 3

2015 57

2016 123

2017 149

2018 203

2019—2020 231

Foreword

Most Houstonians will know the name Leon Hale. Older Texans will remember his name and photograph from *The Houston Post*. Those less old, and even younger, will remember him from the *Houston Chronicle*.

He began writing for a Houston daily newspaper in 1947, when there were still two nice fat ones, stuffed full of information, comics, and sports.

He started out as the *Post's* farm editor, which required him to become acquainted with farmers and ranchers all around Texas. These contacts would serve him well when he began his more general column, and they continued to do so—bolstered by many friends and additional contacts—until he outlived most of them.

By the time he wrote his last column for the *Chronicle* in the spring of 2014, age 93, he had also found time to write eleven books, several of which remain in print.

Hale has been celebrated for his deceptively simple style, gentle humor and deep understanding of the human spirit with all its flaws, quirks and generosities.

A World War II veteran and child of the Great Depression, he nurtures an optimism grounded in the small good things of life, the creatures and experiences that surround us around us daily, if we would only notice.

These qualities remain evident in the pages that follow which end with his entry for the day he began his 100th year.

—*Babette Fraser Hale*
July 28, 2020

See You On Down the Road

Introduction

This is the beginning of what I'm calling a retirement journal. I considered naming it The Last Days of Leon Hale but that seems pretty smart-ass, and might tempt the fates to put an end to me before I finish the first paragraph.

I'm somewhat late getting started on this project and here's why: When I finally quit doing the column I was so fed up with writing sentences I didn't want to produce another, for any reason. I wanted to see what it felt like to live a little while without putting as many as a dozen words together that made sense. And to go to sleep at 11 o'clock without worrying about an idea for the next column.

I've lived that way now for more than three months, and I have enjoyed it ever so much. Sitting on the front porch here at the Winedale place, reading and listening to the birds and doing not one lick of anything kin to working for a newspaper. The only labor of any kind I've done is clean up the kitchen and make up the bed.

So, am I tired of living this way?

Why no, I'm not tired of doing nothing, but I've developed a small problem. I keep hearing this Whisper. Sounds a little like it's coming through my hearing aids when they're not working quite right. The Whisper says, "You ought to be working. You ought to be working. You ought to be working."

OK, so I ought to be working, but at what? I'm simply not ready to pursue the projects I talked about, back before I quit. I said I had part of a play written, and close to a third of a novel, and other unfinished work that would keep me busy until it was time to attend my own funeral. But that work is not exactly beckoning. In fact, I'm not interested in it right now.

But I would like to make that Whisper go away. So I'm starting this journal. It pretends to be work, at least, and I'm somewhat curious about what will show up in it.

—Winedale
June, 2014

2014

14 JUNE

I'm not a stranger to journals. I did a lengthy one about my health adventures, including two surgeries at M.D. Anderson Cancer Clinic, and I had fun with that. (Writing about it was fun, I mean.) It's the only thing I've written in the last twenty years that I really enjoyed. And nobody other than a couple of close friends has read it.

Today, however, when I told Babette I was beginning a journal, she came close to jumping with what I suppose was joy. She is probably tired of me sitting around with my head stuck in a book.

I intend to be easy on myself, in the writing of this stuff. I won't be making an entry every day, or even every week. And I'm not giving it a particular theme or direction, as I did with the medical journal. This one will be about whatever occurs to me when I sit down here to add an entry.

What occurs to me now, on this first day, is that I'm somewhat surprised to be here at age ninety-three, to write a journal or do anything else. When I was in my forties I told Dr. Daniel Gordon Walker I figured I'd die before I was sixty. He had just excavated my right jaw. He laughed at me, about my prediction of making an early exit. Told me what the life expectancy was then for males. I've forgotten the number but it was somewhere near seventy.

Much later on, I was probably pretty close to that age when I ran into Dr. Walker in the Albuquerque Airport. I hadn't seen Walker in more than twenty years and he remembered me talking about dying young, and laughed at me again. I suppose he's dead now but I guess he'd laugh, one more time, if he knew I was here at Winedale typing on a computer keyboard at ninety-three.

I don't recall where I got the idea that I'd die early. Probably it originated with this condemned bone disease, fibrous dysplasia, that came along with me at birth. If that's true, funny thing: I now suspect that the dysplasia may in some mysterious way be a factor in my longevity. No, I've never had a doctor tell me that. I just have a strong suspicion that the condition has somehow kept me alive, maybe so it can maintain its own self by sucking the life out of my bones.

Is it still with me? Oh yes, and going strong. I can feel it now, a slight pain in my right forehead and jaw and eye, plus a vague throbbing itch that says to me, "I'm here, still here, building my bony lesions, doing my damage to your skeleton."

I didn't intend to get started on diseases this early. About time for supper so I'll quit. Angel hair pasta tonight, with pomodoro sauce. M-m-m-m.

19 JUNE

"How do you like retirement?"

I hear that question every day now. I always answer that I like it, which is true. In fact, I like not working better than I thought I would. What's not to like about not working?

I've had a bushel of goodbye mail from the customers, many of whom have been readers since my early days at *The Houston Post*. Our current family doctor, Karen Hoermann, says she began reading the column when she was ten years old. I had a letter from a person who signed his name Buck Forney. Said he was eighty-seven and had been reading my stuff for sixty-two years. And he wondered why I wanted to quit, when he gave the reason in his own letter. Sixty-two years of it, that's why.

A good many of my long-time customers are telling me that I'll miss doing the column. They see me going back to the *Chronicle* pretty soon and asking for my old space. No way. That won't happen. Among my editors at the paper there was talk, when I quit, that I might send in a column now and then, maybe once a month, or twice a year. But they were just being kind. When old hands like me retire, we need to disappear, get out of the way.

We're at Winedale today. Pretty nice weather. Promise of rain. Send it along, please. The spring of 2014 has been good, with lots of moisture, so much that I hear people referring to the drouth in the past tense, as if it's over and we've gone back to the sweet times when we had plenty of water to suit everybody. I hope they're right but I have my doubts. Let's see what happens in July and August and September.

My retirement, after more than sixty years of writing the column, has been a big thing in my life but not the biggest. My main concern the last few months has been Babette's recovery from hip-joint surgery.

One of the reasons I decided to quit work when I did, I wanted to be free to take care of my girl after her operation. You hear people who've had hip-joint replacements say, "Oh, it's a piece of cake." But I figured it wouldn't be easy for Babette and I was right. She's had a lot of serious pain, and I hate that so much.

But I had rather be with her, doing what I can, than to have anybody else trying to care for her. We hired a nurse to come home with us from the hospital. She's a pro and tried hard, but after the first night we sent her back where she came from.

Another nice day, with a surprise shower before noon. About a quarter of an inch. I love rain that simply pops up, without benefit of forecast. Somebody saying, "Hey, it's raining."

We're spending these long days in the country, at the Winedale place. Some of my old newspaper pals ask, "What do you DO up there in the woods?"

For starters, I get up every morning around six, not by choice but because that's when Rosie the Lab comes snarffling up to my bedside and announces that she's got to go out. So before 6:30 I'm in a rocking chair on the front porch, waiting for Rosie to perform.

When she does, I go out and scoop it up, empty it into a small plastic grocery bag, courtesy Round Top Mercantile, tie it up neatly and deposit the package in a thirty-gallon garbage bag hanging on the yard fence.

I do this before breakfast, before coffee, because if I don't, our fenced yard here in the country will be covered in Labrador retriever poop, all of it Rosie's. Four, five times a day. Beats hell out of me where it all comes from. How can a dog poop more than she eats?

By seven o'clock I'm having breakfast on the front porch. Shredded wheat, with sliced banana or red grapes and soy milk. I eat on the porch so I can hear what Babette calls the Dawn Chorus, the brief period early in the day when all the birds sing at once. Babette misses this most mornings because she's still sleeping.

Rosie and I enjoyed a fine Chorus this morning, led by a wren singing so loud and so close that I had to turn down the volume on my hearing aids. We also had a rain crow stop in the big live oak just inside the yard gate and deliver his string of clucks. Rain crows are shy and almost never come in the yard. Something mysterious and significant may be going on, that only the birds know about.

At seven-thirty I feed Rosie. One and a half cups of scientifically balanced dog pellets.

Next we feed the birds, generous handfuls of black oil sunflower seed. I am making progress at my hobby of becoming a bird whisperer.

I use a call that my Aunt Ruth Campbell used long ago to talk to her fat old Rhode Island Red hens. They would come waddling up and stand around Aunt Ruth's feet and talk back to her. "C-a-w, c-a-a-w, c-a-a-a-a-w. . ."

The female cardinals will let me step within eight feet of them now, before they fly. On my best day so far, a red bellied woodpecker clung to a fence post and ate sunflower seed while I stood not four feet away. My goal is to have this beautiful bird eat while perched on my hand or wrist. I may not live long enough to see this, but I think it's good to have a goal, something to move toward.

The reason I feed birds, when I was young I killed a lot of them. Song birds. Any kind of bird. Country boys did that in my growing-up time, getting themselves ready to become hunters, which I never became. I'm trying to be good to birds now. If anybody is keeping records in the Great Book, maybe I'll get credit for this black oil sunflower seed I'm feeding here at Winedale. It costs about twenty bucks for a twenty-five-pound sack.

Let the record show that.

28 JUNE

A bad day at Black Rock. Rosie the Lab has gone to the animal hospital in Brenham. She got hold of something that made her dangerously sick. If this dog dies before she's two years old,

Babette will enter into a prolonged period of grief that I may not survive.

29 JUNE

Nice morning. Three cottontails playing tag on the gravel just inside the front gate.

Dog doctor called around nine A.M. Rosie doing better. Out of danger, apparently. (I am saved.) She must have eaten something extremely toxic. Lord knows we've got a lot of plants around here that aren't supposed to be eaten. But that's a dog for you. Give her scientifically balanced pellets, made by experts in Kansas City especially for a dog of Rosie's breed and weight, and what does she do? Goes out in the pasture and eats poison. This is supposed to be a smart dog.

Back to journaling. Couple of days ago I started talking about what I do on an ordinary day here in the country, and I never got much past breakfast.

After breakfast I clean up the kitchen. Do the dishes, that is, and sweep (sometimes), and carry out the trash. A big truck comes every Tuesday from Sealy to haul away the principal product of our rural acreage—garbage.

So Tuesday is always an important day for me. I have to be up and about and energetic and clear-headed, so I can have my thirty-gallon garbage bags filled and tied off and properly placed just outside the front gate before the truck comes. This is another of the really important things I do now. Just because I'm retired you don't need to think I'm involved totally in trivial pursuits.

My right hearing aid has just now given off a single note. Sounds somewhat like a sedate doorbell chime. This means its battery is about to play out. It also means the battery in my left aid is about to play out, as well, since they both began service at the same time. So, all other activity ceases while I change my batteries.

You might not believe how many hundreds of dollars I have spent over the last five years on hearing aids, so I can hear all available sounds, many of which I don't want to hear in the first place. I am so well acquainted with the ladies at Medical Center Hearing Aid, I get birthday cards from them. If I live two more years, and my hearing continues to deteriorate, I'll be an expert hearing aid mechanic. A deaf one, though.

OK, batteries replaced and I'm hearing again. Fresh batteries certainly enhance my reception. I'm even hearing the mocking-bird singing from the top of the big dead cedar, across the road from us.

Where was I, when the battery alarm interrupted? Oh yes, my daily duties here in the country. I have converted from a pro newspaper columnist to a full-time house husband. And the rea-son is, Babette is still working, writing her stories and managing the affairs she inherited from her family. She's paying most of the biggest bills now, too, so we agreed it would be fair if I took over the housekeeping.

So far, I've not done a very good job of it. Oh, I do the kitchen, and make up the bed, and go to the grocery store, but I don't really keep the house. When I first retired I had big plans. I intended to run this place. Do the laundry. Learn how to cook. And Babette could work full time, which is all she wants to do.

Took me a couple of weeks to see this just wasn't going to hap-pen. Come on, I can't cook for this woman. I can fry eggs and boil pinto beans and that's about it.

So I've left the cooking to Babette. I stay in the kitchen and make favorable remarks about how wonderful everything smells (even though I am unable to smell anything other than a skunk at close range) and I pat her on the behind every time she passes by and after we eat I clean up the mess and feel very fortunate.

I'm doing a lot of itching and scratching this summer, due to chiggers. Redbugs, that is. Got 'em by walking through tall grass and weeds. Those little blood suckers can deal misery. I've been trying to remember what we used to do about chiggers, other than scratch. I remember summers when kids would get so loaded with chiggers their legs would swell up and they'd run a degree or two of fever.

I have learned this fine verse, off the Internet:

> How big was this chigger?
> He wasn't no bigger
> Than half the head of a pen.
> But the bump that he raises,
> It itches like blazes,
> And that's where the rub comes in.

The inside of my thighs, right now, are speckled with flaming chigger bites. Bad timing, because I had to go to M.D. Anderson to have my annual cysto exam, to see whether my bladder cancer is trying to come back. You may not know what a cysto is. If not, I hope you never learn.

The patient receiving a cysto exam has to spread his bare legs, revealing not only the inside of his thighs but everything else in the vicinity that nature provided. And between his knees stands a nurse doing the prep for the test and yes, this is a female nurse.

She said to me, "My Lord, what's this awful rash on your thighs?"

I tell her not to worry, those are just chigger bites.

"What kind of bites?"

I tell her again. Chigger bites. Redbugs.

"BED bugs?!"

No, not bed bugs, RED bugs. I take a minute to explain the role of redbugs in the lives of Texas people, and guess what—she has never heard of a redbug. This is a woman in her forties trained as a technician to work at the world's leading cancer clinic and she doesn't know what a chigger is. During the test she seemed nervous and toward the end she asked if the chiggers could jump off me and onto her. I told her they can't. Actually I don't know if they can or not.

Time for lunch. I'm having a fried egg sandwich. Babette has promised pork tenders for supper, with baked sweet potato.

4 JULY

Here at Winedale my Coca Cola thermometer on the front porch is sitting on eighty-six degrees at one P.M. I'm betting this will be one of the coolest July Fourths on the local weather record. We may even get lucky enough to attract one of those thirty-percent scattered showers popping up here and there.

A nice holiday. Quiet. Babette working on one of her short stories, the dog gone back to bed for most of the day, and I can do what I want.

Feeling pretty good today. Our helper lady in Houston, Maureen Huddleston, put one of her magic bracelets on my wrist about three months ago. Bracelet is supposed to have the effect of "acupuncture without needles." Maureen is involved in the promotion and distribution of this product. As I understand, if acupuncture will successfully treat a disability, this plastic bracelet will do the same, sans needles. I'm not sure what the bracelet is intended to do for me. True, I'm still alive at 93, but I don't know whether this is due to Maureen's magic bracelet or Dr. Hoermann's pills. So far, the bracelet is at least a hell of a lot cheaper.

Daughter Becky called yesterday to announce that she's taking bridge lessons, hoping to get good enough that she can sail away on a bridge-playing cruise. She likes cruises. She should do well at that game. Her mother was a whiz of a bridge player.

Mark, her brother, has gone to Alabama, as we understand, to help his son Daniel get a house ready to sell. Mark's golf course, where he has worked mostly for the past year, is closed and being redesigned.

Getting back to what I do out here in the country, after I finish making up the bed and policing the kitchen, I rest. I now do almost no physical labor out here, other than picking up dog poop and killing snakes. I'm not even allowed to replace a light bulb if it means getting on a ladder.

I used to mow this entire place on a ten-horse John Deere riding mower. I liked doing that. I dug and fertilized Babette's flower garden. I raised a few vegetables. Did simple repairs. Stayed busy.

Now I do none of that, because of the case of atrial fibrillation I've developed in my heart, along with the aortic aneurysm I've had probably fifteen years. I know, people live for decades with those heart problems but they make me close to useless. I've got no stamina. I take a little bucket of birdseed fifty steps to the back of the yard and by the time I feed the birds and return to the front porch, I'm pooped and puffing. I walk the dog, slowly, down to the tank to feed my fish and when I get back I collapse, as if I've just run a 100-yard dash.

I do recover pretty fast.

On this holiday we used to go into Round Top and join in the old-fashioned Fourth of July Celebration that's been held in that little town ever since Romeo met Juliet. They have a parade and patriotic speeches and barbecue and dancing and they fire a damn cannon that lives on the town square and that's why I didn't want to go this year. I am no longer attracted, as I once was, to loud explosive noise. Hurts my ears. Jolts my blood pressure. Startles my A-fibbed heart.

In times past I always went to Round Top on the Fourth. But that was when I could drink beer all day and dance 'til the band quit and get up the next morning and go to work, laughing at a hangover. I believe even a moderate hangover would now kill me.

A while ago I had the TV on and there was a crowd scene shot in San Francisco and I saw a guy in the multitude who looked like Vincent Scatena. It couldn't have been Vince because this guy was young and Vince would be at least ninety years old if he's alive. He was waist gunner on our B-24 crew in Italy during WWII.

In recent years I keep seeing faces in crowds that resemble faces of that crew. I shared with those guys a year of combat in Europe, when we felt like brothers having the most intense of human experiences. Early in May of 1945 when the shooting was over, we hugged one another and said goodbye and swore we'd stay in touch and get together at least once a year as long as we lived.

But I've never received as much as a postcard from one of them, and I've made no attempt to keep track, either. That seems so strange to me now. I've thought of trying to find them. The Internet has made it possible to locate almost anybody, so I might be successful. But I'm afraid I'd simply discover that they're all dead. If they're not, maybe they're thinking the same about me.

15 JULY

For Babette's 70th birthday (July 12th) we were all stirred up about going to New York, so she could celebrate with her only grandchild. But as the departure date came near, both of us began having doubts about the trip.

Mainly because we've lost the capability to walk long distances. And if you can't walk, there's not much point in going to NY. Babette's walking problem is, we hope, temporary, a side effect of her hip surgery. Mine, I feel sure, is permanent, on account of my age. I feel as if my knees, and most of my other joints, have simply worn out.

In any event I can't walk well and neither can Babette, so we cancelled the New York plane tickets and the hotel reservations, put the dog in the kennel, and went instead to San Antonio. Got into a fancy hotel on the Riverwalk, stayed four nights, ate expensive room service meals, and had a great time without walking more than two blocks in any direction.

We always do well in San Antonio. It's the nearest we can come to returning to Santa Fe, which is where we'd most like to go. But we can't because that 7,200-foot elevation pushes my blood pressure off the top of the scale. Is that enough irony for you? The city we yearn to visit—possibly live in—is just one good day's drive away, and it won't accept us.

Santa Fe is where Babette and I happened. Before Santa Fe, my feeling was, come on, this can't be serious. This beautiful, educated young woman, twenty-three years younger than I, she's just off on a lark with an older guy. She's a writer. She's gathering material.

But I decided, What the hell, I'll enjoy it while it lasts. It was a kick for me, to walk into a restaurant or any crowded place with this lovely young woman. I'd say silently, "How about this, guys? This is not my daughter. This is not my niece. This is my girl."

She knew things I didn't know, and I knew things she didn't know. We danced, and sang songs. We cooked. We travelled. We worked together. We made love, you bet, and this went on for weeks and weeks, months.

Then one day in Santa Fe, up on the side of a mountain, it struck me—hey, this is not going away. This is serious. I have fooled around and flat fallen in love with this young woman.

And it scared me. I didn't know what to think about it. Babette says now that she knew it long before I did, and she was sure about it and comfortable with it from the start.

I wasn't convinced. We talked. Even argued. Look, I'd say, do the math. When I'm a slobbery eighty-year-old man, unable to work or walk or make love, she'd be an attractive fifty-seven-year-old chick who'll still want to go out and about on Saturday night, and horny guys sixty years old will be hitting on her.

But that didn't bother her. She'd laugh about it. She'd say that since we loved one another, and got along well together, it seemed to her the thing to do was stay together, whether we ever got married or not.

So together we stayed, for the longest time.

We bought things together and they became our things. We bought a dog. We bought furniture. We bought these ten acres of woods at Winedale, Texas, and made a home here.

We got to know married couples who seemed less married than we were, so one day we stood up before the fireplace in Babette's house in River Oaks and said the words before my preacher friend, David Horsley out of Amarillo. With Mark and Becky and Will as witnesses. Afterward I felt good but I didn't feel much different. It was like we'd been married a long time.

Let's see, about 32 years have passed now since Babette and I met, and when we walk together into a crowded place—I'm ninety-three and she's seventy and beautiful as ever—I still feel the words inside me, pushing to come out, loud and clear:

"How about this, guys? This is my girl."

Well, I just now read over a few previous entries and they sound more like a history than a journal. I'll try to be more daily.

This is a Sunday, and a torrid one. Still, you hear people saying we've had a nice summer, so far. That's because the last few years have been so drouthy, with summer temps up in the triple digits. This year we haven't yet had a 100-degree day and here we are in the last week of July.

Went into Round Top early this morning and brought back a supply of hot biscuits and pancakes from Scotty's Restaurant. Scotty packages these breakfast treats in a way that they can be frozen and we can thaw 'em out and have biscuits and pancakes several mornings, off that one order. Not as good as fresh, of course, but good enough.

Not that I mind going to town, for any reason, if I can go in my pickup. Sometimes I go when I don't need to. Five miles into Round Top. Or eight miles into Carmine. Or ten into Burton or even twenty-five or thirty into Brenham or La Grange. I don't need much of an excuse to crank up the truck.

Sometimes when we suffer through a long siege of extra hot or extra cold weather, I can get tired staying in this old house. But I've never grown tired of driving the country roads in this part of the world. Every time I drive to town I see things I love, no matter how many times I've seen them before.

A whitetail doe crossing the road ahead of me, followed by a fawn. A neighbor walking out to her mailbox, to see what the carrier has left. A hawk, hovering over a fresh-cut meadow, hunting his breakfast. A jackrabbit sailing across the blacktop. A few tricky notes floating into my window from a mockingbird. A new calf, running circles around its mama. A farmer waving from his tractor. These kinds of things are important to me. They're genuine. They tell me we're in a good place, that we did the right thing, buying this little patch of woods and putting so much of ourselves into it.

28 JULY

A Monday, my favorite day of the week here at Winedale. Because on Monday all the weekend farmers have already gone back to Houston and Austin, to make more money so they can afford to come back next Friday.

I've convinced myself that I can feel the countryside heave a relaxing sigh Monday mornings.

The weekends here can get what you'd almost call hectic, especially in the spring when the tourists are running up and down the roads looking for bluebonnets.

And the weekend farmers have invited their neighbors and kinfolks, to give them a taste of country living. Then we have our special weekends, like the big antique shows, and sometimes even on our little road the dust doesn't settle from Friday until dark on Sunday.

But Monday morning, it's all gone. It's like a mantle of near-silence has settled on the land. I like to get a cup of coffee early Monday and sit out on the front porch and count the traffic. Sometimes, no more than six vehicles will pass our front gate between six and eight A.M. If I were in Houston during those two hours, looking down on San Felipe from our apartment balcony, I'd get cross-eyed trying to count the cars going by. But it pleases me to think about that contrast.

Babette fusses at me a little because I always sit on the front porch, rather than the back. In the back we face a solid stand of woods and the bird- and animal-watching is better. I've tried to make the switch to the back porch but for some reason I like to face the road, even when nothing much is going by. I guess a shrink could get an hour's work out of that.

Maybe it traces back to my father, who always wanted to face the road, to see who was passing, who they were, and where they were going, and why.

Had a nice rain shower late this afternoon. Measured nine-tenths of an inch. Some of the old dudes at the Post Office would say the shower gave us more than an inch because "the wind blew a lot of it over the top of the gauge." You hear that expression mainly from the locals, about wind blowing rain over the top of the gauge so that we don't get an accurate reading. I don't know what to think about that.

2 AUGUST

Drove into Brenham this morning to pick up a few groceries at HEB and a supply of pills at the drugstore. HEB recently tore its store down and put it back together as one hell of a huge enterprise, with a monster of a wine section. I even found a bottle of Chicken Run cabernet in there, for ten bucks. I think it was my old friend George Fuermann who introduced me to Chicken Run.

It comes from Chile. George was big on Chilean wines. The claim is that Chicken Run is made from grapes grown organically, with pest control done by chickens roaming the vineyards. I don't understand how chickens could eat everything that pesters grape vines but I like the story, and I like the wine.

3 AUGUST

Finding the Chicken Run has led me into my drinking history, which starts with a bottle of Muelebach beer in Breckenridge,

Texas in 1939. And lasts through about 6 P.M. yesterday when I finished my glass of cabernet.

That's what I drink now—one glass of red wine daily. Or one bottle of beer. If I have the beer I don't get the wine. Where I come from, that's pretty close to total abstinence.

Reason behind this harsh limitation is, I've just about been convinced that I'm an alcoholic. If not I'm surely pretty close. I have, in fact, stood up in AA meetings and said the words. "My name is Hale and I'm an alcoholic." And I've listened to all those folks spin stories about destroying their lives with alcohol and drugs. And in those meetings I've told a story or two about my own boozing.

But even while I was doing that, I wasn't entirely convinced that I'm truly alcoholic.

Oh, I don't deny that I have mighty strong symptoms. Back when I was doing the daily column, working mostly at home, I'd often open a beer at 10 o'clock in the morning, and another one at noon, and keep a tiny little buzz going most of the day. I thought it helped me write better sentences. This became fairly standard for me, writing when I was just a bit tight. In the '70s I wrote my beer-joint novel, *Bonney's Place*, in what I called spare time, and I doubt a page of that story was written when I was totally sober. Not drunk, though.

In Bryan, when I was going to church regularly and raising children and coaching Little League baseball, I once overheard a Baptist lady say about me, "I've never seen him when I didn't think he was half drunk."

Maybe I deserved that, but this cursed disease, fibrous dysplasia, has done things to my face, especially my eyes, that make me look somewhat weird and not exactly normal. So maybe a Baptist lady might interpret that look as being common to drunks.

I've seen this in photographs, taken of me when I know I wasn't drunk. Looking kind of cock-eyed. Oh well.

Going through two divorces within a five-year period didn't do a lot to sober me up. And yet, I've never disappeared on five-day drunks. I've never walked wobbly into the newsroom. I've always done my work. I've simply felt a little better if I was slightly tight.

When I ended up, twice divorced, in Treetops Apartments around 1980, that's when my drinking became the worst. And I did have two or three close calls, when driving.

So I've been lucky.

Treetops was occupied by two kinds of people—those who partied all the time, and those who had already partied too much and had quit and joined AA. I got acquainted there with a few pure-bred and registered alcoholics. I recall sweating through a hangover one morning and I remarked to a bottle-scarred neighbor that I was afraid I'd become an alcoholic. He asked, "Do you wake up every morning wanting a drink, more than orange juice or coffee?" I told him no, never, and he said, "Then you ain't no alcoholic." That has since been a mild comfort to me. Here at least was one genuine drunk who didn't think I was alcoholic.

I was living at Treetops when I met Babette. She would eventually help me control my drinking but not immediately. In our early association we'd normally have a drink or two—gin or vodka—and then split a bottle of wine at dinner and go to bed pretty well juiced. Today Babette doesn't drink at all. She quit, cold turkey. She became unable to drink because alcohol made her feel perfectly terrible instead of better.

My worst experience with booze happened in Santa Fe, where we had bought a neat adobe-style house and were trying to live in New Mexico part-time. After an evening of drinking that was still standard for me at the time, I was awakened about 2:30 a.m. by something alarming going on in my chest.

My heart was way off rhythm, something like an old gasoline engine with the cylinders firing out of sequence. This wasn't especially painful but it was scary. I woke Babette and she hauled me to the hospital in my pajamas. That hospital wasn't known for its excellence but the docs on duty in the ER knew what to do in my case. I had a serious case of atrial fibrillation and they gave me medicine that controlled it quickly.

I spent one night in that hospital, came out sober, and for the next five years I didn't have one drink, not even a short beer.

I can't say I really suffered during those dry years but I sure as hell got tired of them. I went to cocktail parties and sipped ice water and tried to pass it off as gin on the rocks. I endured everlasting dinner parties where all the other guests sat at table long after dessert, and sipped wine, and laughed over stories and remarks that to me were not funny. During my five years of total sobriety we spent a month in France, down south in all that beautiful wine country. It seemed to me everybody we met on that trip had a drink in hand.

I went five times on a fishing/camping trip to the Texas Hill Country with a gang of friends, and in that gang everybody except me DID have a drink in hand. These were guys I'd known for decades, and I felt like a stranger among them.

I was asked, I bet a hundred times, "Do you miss not drinking?" And a hundred times I answered, "Yes."

When I was creeping up on my ninetieth birthday, it was decided that one glass of red wine daily might be beneficial to my health, provided it would not lead me back into my alcoholic ways to become a hopeless drunk. I say "it was decided" because I don't remember who made the decision. Babette, I guess. Maybe Dr. Hoermann, too, even though she is a teetotaler.

Whoever made the decision, I was ever so pleased it was made.

Of course I heard warnings. Beware, one small drink of beer, whiskey, wine, gin or vodka can be poisonous to an alcoholic.

Did these warnings deter me? No.

I began with about two ounces of cabernet. Took it down in tiny, careful sips. Sat back and waited. Would I be seized by a desperate hankering for two more ounces? For four more? For the entire bottle?

Nothing like that came to pass. But in a few minutes, I was delighted to feel just a hint of a tiny inner glow, the tingling warmth that I knew and loved from my drinking days, and which I had not felt in five years. I was astonished to get that small buzz from just two ounces of red wine.

Wow. What might a full glass of wine do for me?

I went to Google to see how much wine is in a glass. The American Medical Association and other respected sources consider that a glass of wine holds five ounces. The standard bottle holds 25 ounces, or five glasses.

So I began taking a five-ounce drink once a day, before dinner, with Babette as a critical witness. That glass of the grape before dinner has become dear to me. It gives me a moderate glow that lasts maybe 10 minutes. I love that tiny buzz. I look forward to it daily. If I don't get it, yes, I miss it but I don't throw a trembling fit about it.

If I'm a true alcoholic, shouldn't one glass of wine make me want a second, and a third, and a fourth? This hasn't happened yet, and I've been on this one-drink-a-day schedule for two years. The only time I want a second glass is when we're out, say with friends, and everybody else is drinking, and an hour or more has passed since I had my one glass. I recall having that second glass on two occasions, while Babette was hitting me with her stare of disapproval. That message, along with the tenth ounce of caber-

net, did not make me feel any better. I think a third or a fourth
glass would probably put me to sleep at the table.

5 AUGUST

Our friend Clinton, who drives a big UPS van on these country
roads, just delivered a rescue package from Maureen in Houston. It contained two copies of *The New Yorker*, one of *National
Geographic* and a two-week-old *Sunday Times*. I love it when the
package brings us two copies of the *New Yorker*. When we get
only one, we flip to see who gets it first, and I always lose.

Chicken fajitas for supper. Not bad.

27 AUGUST

Here we are in the depths of the dog days—the last week of
August. This is when Texas weather is so often at its worst, and
we've had a bitter taste of it here at Winedale lately. No significant rain for weeks. Not much wind, and the countryside enters
into a sort of coma. Still green and alive, but not active. Foliage
on our trees hangs absolutely still. Day-time temps into triple
digits. The dog sleeps all day. Right now she's curled up in the
bathtub, empty except for Rosie.

But it's raining in Houston, 90 miles southeast. A tropical-type
weather system is moving east to west across the northern Gulf,
giving the TV meteorologists the opportunity to announce, one
more time, that they will keep an eye on it. Maybe we'll get some
moisture out of that system. Our tank needs it. Babette needs it.
Her dog needs it. Her husband needs it. His pickup needs it.

Speaking of the tank, that body of water right now doesn't even
look wet. Somebody has thrown a ragged, sick-green blanket of
what we call moss over its surface. I've got 150 young hybrid sun

fish in the tank. I pitch pellets of food to them every few days but
I can't see them because of that cover of acquatic vegetation. Are
they eating? Growing? *Quien sabe*.

Mike Robison, runs a fish farm north of Brenham, is trying
to find me a supply of young tilapia, to put in the tank. They're
vegetarians. Live on acquatic plants. I'm hot to see if they'd eat
that green blanket.

That voice you hear in the background is Babette, talking on
the phone about Friends of Winedale, an organization I suspect is
about to become highly influential in my life. It already is, in hers.

Winedale Historical Center is a neighbor of ours. It's owned
by the University of Texas which has let it go to hell, or close.
Fences falling down. Buildings need repairing. A small group
of folks, most of whom live or own property in this area, have
formed a non-profit corporation, Friends of Winedale. Its aim is
to raise money to benefit the historical center, to return it to the
fine facility it was before UT quit caring about it.

Is Babette involved in this organization? Well, yes, she's the
president of it. She had a lot to do with putting the group together.
I sat here and heard her do it, mostly on the phone. She is good
at that sort of thing. I've always said she could talk a skunk into
smelling nice.

Weather.com's radar is now showing a nice green glob passing
right over this house, so we ought to be getting rain but we're not.
We do have a cloud cover which has driven the temp down a few
notches, so thanks for that.

30 AUGUST

Still no rain after days of wet clouds passing us by.

I'm missing the mockingbird. Most of this summer we had a
hard-working mocker singing all day and part of the night from

the top of a big dead cedar just across the road. Bird has gone silent now. Guess it raised a family, or accomplished whatever it was singing about, and moved on. I especially enjoyed this particular mocker because it was able to produce the chatter of a scissortail, which is one of my favorite of all bird calls, and we don't have scissortails on or near our place.

Babette breezed by my desk and left me a small treat—a bowl of fresh peaches. She'd just finished peeling and slicing them. We bought this fruit a few days ago in Brenham and it was then hard as an oak knot. But a short stay in the kitchen and Wow, its flavor and texture is flat scrumtiferous. (Is that a word? Well, it is now.)

The mention of peaches causes the calm face of Fred Muegge to appear before me. He and I were members of a group of friends who camped and fished on the James River in Mason County. The others of us took hamburger meat to fry there on the river, and bacon, and beans. Fred? He'd bring delicious peaches, or a big bag of vine-ripe tomatoes.

Fred is dead. I hate so much to type those words. Killed by one of those evil blood diseases that can't be cured, and he couldn't have been fifty. He loved things of the earth, and lived as close to nature as anyone I know.

One of the negatives of having ninety-odd birthdays is that you have to watch so many of your younger friends die. Fred and I had a common good friend in Bill Shearer, the Texas book publisher, and even Bill is gone, taken away by a brain tumor at forty-six.

1 SEPTEMBER

About 7:30 this morning I was up at the front gate and our neighbor Mark Fiedler came jogging along the road. He stopped and said he was hearing dove hunters shooting. Told him to keep his head down. He grinned and jogged off.

Dove season. I hadn't thought about it. Here at Winedale we're in the central zone of the state where the season opens today. I haven't heard any shooting yet.

When we first got this place we heard gunfire every day, hunting season or not. But population of the neighborhood has increased now to the point that you need to be careful about which way you're shooting, or you might hit a neighbor. Especially if you're firing a rifle.

Our neighbor to the north, Randon Dillingham, is an expert with a shotgun. I've seen him shoot skeet off the deck of his house, and he is a whiz at it. But now that I think of it, I haven't lately heard him fire a shot. He's recently married a red-headed schoolteacher. Maybe she doesn't like loud noises.

Then our neighbor to the south, Henry Ullrich, has a firing range out behind his house. Every now and then he loads all his guns and it's blim blam boom bam for maybe an hour until he runs out of ammo. But he is an excellent neighbor with a fine green tractor and he'll come pull my pickup out of a mudhole, or hook up his shredder and mow our pasture, or perform any other job that makes a great noise.

We have guns, sure. We have a 20-gauge shotgun and a .22 pistol and several boxes of bullets lost somewhere in the bedroom closet. The shotgun has been fired twice in its life. Babette shot a large armadillo off the front porch in 1988, I think it was, and promised never to do anything like that again because it made, in the armadillo, such a large unsightly hole.

A few years later I used the shotgun to slay another dillo in the back yard. I think Babette fired the .22 pistol down on the tank a couple of times. I've never fired it myself. But you see we are armed and ready when the terrorists attack. If we can find the ammo.

Some of our closest neighbors are pairs of nice ladies who, I'm pretty sure, are opposed to violence and wouldn't care to shoot anybody (except maybe Pam just across the road). Kathy and Priscilla have a fine little house on about twenty acres, to the south of us. Leslie and Cathy live up on the blacktop a mile north, where mesquite trees grow.

Pam and Carol lived just across the road from us until recently. They sold their place and moved away and we miss them fiercely. What fine neighbors they were. When we had a construction project going on here and the house wasn't livable, Pam and Carol gave us a key to their place and we stayed over there several nights. And now they're gone.

Getting on with the neighbors, we have Don Stewart and his wife, who bought "the yonder house" from the Dillinghams. So they're just the other side of Randon and Laura.

Don likes to burn off his pasture to make the grass comes back greener. One day we had a gathering of neighbors at his place when he had a burn-off planned. I attended, with my cell phone fully charged so I could call the volunteer fire department in case he set half the county ablaze.

Stewart assigned me to a golf cart with a water tank on it, and a squirting device to douse flames that threatened to get out of control. I enjoyed doing that, and when nobody was looking I zipped around putting out fires that were not yet out of control.

Across the road from Stewart lives another of our close neighbors, by the name of Parks. We don't know them. I have never even seen the Parkses. The most intimate thing I know about them is that on Tuesday mornings they always put just one bag of garbage out on the road for the truck to pick up. This is passing strange to me. Any respectable family ought to be producing more garbage than that.

Two other neighbors we'd call close are the Fiedler brothers, Dennis and Mark. They are friendly gentlemen, and keep their place mowed and neat, with all plants arranged in straight lines and sharp corners. Mark jogs every weekend morning. He always starts at the same time, and runs the same route at the same speed.

For supper tonight? Fried chicken and mashed potatoes from JW's Steak House in Carmine. JW has this FC every Tuesday, no matter what the weather is. We have sworn not to eat fried foods any longer but JW's FC doesn't count because we peel the skin off and throw it away. The skin is where the grease and salt are. That's what we've heard anyway. We still fry eggs but in olive oil that's not only virginal but extra virginal. That term, extra virginal, always reminds me of a girl I dated in high school.

4 SEPTEMBER

Hey, a nice thing has happened. The Press Club of Houston has established a Leon Hale Scholarship Program. This is an honor and I am pleased about it. I think this is a one-time proposition. That is, someone else will be named for the honor each year. But I was first. I like being first.

We attended the banquet where this scholarship deal was announced. It was held at Brady's Landing, a large restaurant serving bad food. You can sit in Brady's so close to an anchored ship that you seem to be dining aboard a luxury liner, except the anchored vessel is a giant tanker tied up in the stinky Houston Ship Channel.

Still, I enjoy that part of Houston. It's like another City. No, another country, another world. Native Houstonians grow up and get old in the residential forests of the West Side and never see the Turning Basin, or any other Houston industrial feature.

When I was living in Bryan and doing the column daily, in the '60s and '70s, now and then I'd wander down into the Ship Channel neighborhood and write about the scene. It was pure-dee scary.

I always thought the last two blocks of 75th Street, on the Channel, made up the sleaziest, most dangerous neighborhood in Houston, and maybe in Texas. Nothing but barny joints on both sides of the street. Bars and whore houses, to empty the pockets of sailors coming off long womanless, boozeless voyages.

I liked to drive slowly along that stretch of 75th, trying to keep a policeman in sight. You could get murdered there. A Houston policeman told me one time that some cops would not accept patrol duty in that neighborhood, or at least didn't want to. Maybe you heard the popular joke about the fellow who walked into a joint on 75th and the bouncer stopped him at the door and asked, "Do you have a knife on you?" The fellow answered, "Why no." And the bouncer asked, "Do you want to buy one?"

5 SEPTEMBER

I woke up this morning thinking about our friend Glenn White-head. Why I don't know. Whitehead is one of the world's dedicated eccentrics. A pure-bred alcoholic, too. I would estimate that he has not been totally sober for the last forty years.

Before he quit traveling he'd go with our fishing/camping bunch on the James River and every year he'd tell his favorite joke when we gathered around the campfire. Same story, just as if all of us hadn't heard it a dozen times. I can forgive him that, though. What I can't forgive is the way he'd sneak chopped bell peppers into my pot of pinto beans. C'mon, Glenn, BELL peppers?

6 SEPTEMBER

A pretty fair Saturday morning. Facebookers and blog posters in Amarillo are bragging about their weather. They've had a front that pushed through and ran the temp down to fifty-four degrees. They got a good inch of rain, too.

Babette is today having her first board of directors meeting of Friends of Winedale. I'm proud of her because she and a couple of other women here in the neighborhood put that organization together and it's getting lots of notice in Houston and Austin papers. It could achieve something of real significance to Texas culture. I could almost go ahead and say Babette put the thing together by herself. She had the idea and she rounded up most of the volunteers to serve as board members and they're off to an impressive start.

What I don't like about it is the stress it puts on her. Stress so often makes her feel punk physically and keeps her upset and I hate that.

15 SEPTEMBER

This is Sister Ima Ruth's birthday. She's ninety-six, and living in a big house in a little town the name of which I can never remember. One of those spin-off towns between Fort Worth and Dallas. Also in that house are her daughter Sandi and her grandson Shawn and his wife and their kids.

Here's what it's like now, talking on the phone with Ima Ruth. I called her this morning.

Me: Hello. This is your brother.

IR: Well.

Me: I just called to wish you a happy birthday.

IR: Hello?

Me: Are you doing anything special for your birthday?

IR: No.

Me: Sandi's making you a birthday cake, I bet.

IR: She's gone to the grocery store.

Me: Are you getting any birthday cards from your friends?

IR: No.

Me: Well, one advantage you have, your grandkids live right there in the house with you, so they don't have to make a long trip to come see you on your birthday.

IR: Yeah.

Me: How are you feeling today?

IR: What?

Me: Are you well?

IR: They're pretty bad.

Me: Who's pretty bad?

IR: That's what I say. They're in the cellar.

    (I figured out she was talking about the Texas
    Rangers. She's a fan of that baseball club.)

Me: Well, there's always next year.

IR: What happened?

Me: I said maybe your team will do better next year.

IR: On my next birthday I'll be ninety-seven.

Me: Say, you won't believe who I ran into the other day, and she asked about you. Marilyn Cunningham. Remember her? You worked a while for her dad, had the real estate office just off the square?

IR: You ought to see Jan and Jodie's house. It's got a swimming pool in the front yard.

Me: Anyway, she said tell you hello.

IR: Who?

Me: Marilyn Cunningham.

IR: Law, no, Mr. Cunningham died I reckon thirty years ago.

Me: Yeah, but he had a daughter, Marilyn. Wasn't she in your class?

IR: He was a good man, I'll say that. I used to work for him.

Me: I guess I'll let you go. I just wanted to wish you a happy birthday.

IR: Now who is this?

OK, so that's stretching it a little, but not a lot. On other days I can get her on the phone and she's bright as a shoe-shine and talks clearly about people and events in our lives that I don't even remember.

This is the person who could once play a thousand songs on the piano, and sing the lyrics to them all.

23 SEPTEMBER

We're in Austin for a few days. I'm sitting on the sixteenth floor of the Hyatt Regency and Babette has gone to a meeting with some University of Texas people about her Friends of Winedale organization.

This hotel is on the west bank of the Colorado and I have a nice scene from my window. A huge swan floats on the river just below me, and fish of some kind break the water occasionally around that big bird, which pays them no attention whatever. Probably they're gars, or some other kind of rough fish. I'm told the river along here is well polluted from the septic systems of residences in the hills west of town.

Speaking of residences, if I were on the other side of the river I could probably see the top of the hill where the Livelys used to live. Jan and Ken. He was editor of *Texas Parade* magazine and I used to sell him a story half a dozen times a year, for the staggering sum of around $25 bucks each.

When I came to Austin I'd get a bottle of Evan Williams bourbon, which the Livelys liked because the label looked like Jack Daniel's. I'd go out to the house and we'd burn some steaks and then go to the living room where they had a fine piano. Ken could play anything on the piano, the same as Ima Ruth, except he needed music to read.

Anyway, Ken would play and Jan and I stood behind him and we all sang. We'd sing for hours. Our friendship seemed to be based on those singing evenings, even more than on the magazine connection. Our specialty was "Where have all the flowers gone. . . ?"

I could pick up this phone right now and call the Livelys and start singing that song and they would know who I was and we haven't talked in ten years. They live now in Dallas, if they're still alive. I don't call because I might find out that they're gone, and if they are I don't want to know it.

29 SEPTEMBER

The 29th? Could that be right? October's sitting right around the corner, so we've survived the quickest September in the history of calendars. September used to be a slow month for me and now it's fast. The world is so full of mysteries.

Tacos for supper. Made with ground buffalo. M-m-m.

30 SEPTEMBER

Here's an e-mail from my old pal, Guy "Dude" Wilkins. He checks my blog every few weeks, to see if I'm still alive. He has just turned ninety-four, plays golf several times a week, and still works. He has done well by becoming an expert in the harvest of salt. Invented a machine that scoops it up in remote places, and until recent times he traveled, all over the planet, doing this salt thing.

It's strange, thinking about Dude as a world traveler (or even a golfer) because when we were in high school I thought of him as my backwoods-type friend. He was even more countrified than I was. Which was pretty countrified, considering that I was daily seen in Eastland leading milk cows around, looking for a johnson grass lot to stake them out on to graze.

Dude loved to fish and hunt and camp out and roam around in the boondocks. In summer when we were fourteen, maybe fifteen, and the temp was 103 degrees, we'd walk all day through the mesquite pastures of Eastland County, exploring. Just messing around. Walk along the railroad. Chunk the glass insulators on the telephone poles. Put a penny on the track when we heard a freight coming. Find an old house, abandoned out in the country, walk through every room, talk about the lives of people who lived there, and the things they left behind. Swim naked in rain-filled slush pits.

We fished a lot, mostly on Eastland Lake. Leave Dude's house before daylight, carrying nothing to eat but three or four of yesterday's biscuits. Seine crawdads for bait, catch channel cats on cane poles. Get thirsty, drink out of the lake. Why not? It was the city's source of drinking water. Never mind that it hadn't yet gone through the municipal purification system.

When Dude turned sixteen his Dad let him hunt with his twenty-two target rifle. The first gun I ever shot. I loved it. We killed anything that moved. Once we killed three or four blue jays and built a fire and cooked them. They tasted awful but we said they were good.

I could write fifty more pages about the adventures Dude and I had, before we discovered girls. Our lives changed after that. We remained friends but we spent more time in town, and took on temporary jobs to make the money needed to take a girl to the picture show and buy her a Coke at the Corner Drugstore.

I'm hungry. Let's quit.

2 OCTOBER

Had an e-mail yesterday from Tim Vick, just a short hello-and-how-are-you. Of all members of Helen's family, Tim is one of three people I have loved and felt close to. The other two are

Mimi and Johnny Green. When Johnny was three or four years old, before Mark was born, he was a really sweet little kid and I would have taken him in a split minute for my own, to raise.

But he has not kept up with me like Tim has. Every few months Tim will check in, make sure we're OK, let us know he's thinking about us. When Babette threw my big ninetieth birthday party at Round Top, Tim attended and so did Johnny Green, all the way from Bastrop, Louisiana. I know why Johnny was there. It was because Tim got on the horn and talked him into it. Maybe went and got him, for all I know.

Babette's laboring men were here today to move the furniture off the porches, both front and back, clearing the deck for the construction project due to start in another week. We're gonna close in, with glass, half the front porch and all the back. Give us some room to spread out. This old house is about to sink into the earth, it's so loaded down with furniture and things, things, things.

What little work I do now is done in the living room. When the front porch project is done, I'll have a separate room, maybe with a day bed. I might end up sleeping on the porch because my snoring and my pitching and rolling around in bed has become a little too much for Babette to put up with, although she doesn't complain.

Reason for the glass walls, I've been sitting out on that front porch for twenty-odd years, looking for whatever moves, and I don't want to give that up. I've seen some worthwhile things out there.

I've seen a big chicken hawk swoop down and grab a field rat, right there in the front yard. I've seen a bobcat walk through our front gate. Hummingbirds, performing their mating flight. Great horned owls. Roadrunners. Once a female donkey, escaped from a neighbor's pasture. A lost dog, accompanied by a Spanish goat.

And I've listened to the voices of the coyotes and horny bulls and mockingbirds and wild geese and sandhill cranes.

This morning at dawn we had four whitetails grazing on our slope, between the house and the front gate. They look nice and fat and healthy. And wild.

Couple of days ago I was talking here about temporary jobs boys worked at, there in Eastland, when I was in high school. One of the strangest I had was jerking soda at Tombs and Richardson Drugstore on the east side of the square. Eastland had three drugstores then. Corner Drug was the most popular of the three. The kids hung out there. Just across Highway 80 was Eastland Drug but nobody ever gathered there like the kids did at Corner Drug.

Tombs and Richardson was a big store, loaded with bottled and packaged merchandise, looked like it had been on the shelves since the store opened. Very little of it ever moved because the store simply had no customers. Beats hell out of me how the place made a living for two families, if it did.

It had a full pharmacy across the back, and a long soda fountain, and a nest of little round tables with wire-back chairs, meant for the fountain trade. In all the time I worked there, two people came in and sat in those chairs to be served. Of course I remember them. They were Julia Parker and Alma Williamson, both my friends from school. They each ordered fountain Cokes. Their total bill was 10 cents.

They never came back because that store was like going in a funeral parlor. Nobody ever talked. The only time I can remember being spoken to by the owners, Mr. Richardson told me how to sell condoms. He said his wife, who worked in there as a clerk, didn't like to sell rubbers (I don't think we knew the word condom then). He said if Mrs. Richardson ever told me to wait on a customer, it was because he wanted rubbers. We had only one kind, and they were Trojans and kept in this drawer right here.

But as far as I know, nobody ever came in wanting rubbers.

We were supposed to have curb service. Some days I'd work a 12-hour shift and not a car would honk for curb service. I remember one day a person pulled up and honked and I went forth and a woman stuck her head out the window and said, "I want the blue box." That didn't sound like a fountain drink order to me. I asked her to repeat and she said again that she wanted the blue box. I went back in and told Mrs. Richardson a lady was out there wanting a blue box and she said, "I'll take care of it."

She went behind the counter and wrapped up a box of Kotex, which was kept out of sight, under a counter. She secured the package with string like it was a Christmas present, and handed it to me along with a look that said, "Just take this out to the car and keep your mouth shut."

I made seventeen and a half cents an hour working at that strange place. Later on I worked part-time at Corner Drug where I made twenty cents an hour, and had a good time because that's where all the girls came to drink their nickel Cokes.

Take-out for supper. Grilled salmon and rice from J.W.'s Steakhouse in Carmine. A good dish because an order of J.W.'s salmon is enough for four people and we get several meals off two orders.

13 OCTOBER

A Monday morning and it's raining. The porch project was due to begin today but looks like it's rained out. So be it. Rather have the rain than the new room.

I was just now reading over the last few entries and they've still got me thinking about Eastland, and the jobs I had there in the '30s. The best one I had was delivery boy for Western Union.

I learned a lot about people in that job, especially about the troubles they were having, and how they handled them. Money troubles, mostly. I stood behind the telegraph operator and watched the messages come in on the yellow tape so I knew who was wiring home for money and what kind of mess they were in. I knew delicate things about families that nobody else knew, other than the families themselves, and the Western Union operator.

On my bicycle I delivered a lot of death messages. In those times, a family didn't want to see the Western Union delivery boy pedaling up their driveway because a telegram was almost always bad news. GROVER DIED THURSDAY STOP FUNERAL 2 OCLOCK SUNDAY PIONEER BAPTIST CHURCH; Or, MAMA WORSE IN HOSPITAL FT WORTH CAN YOU COME.

Then I worked for James Turk Pipkin at the Piggly Wiggly, sacking potatoes mostly. And carrying double armloads of groceries home for old ladies who didn't have cars. Some lived three, four blocks from the store.

Saddest job I had in Eastland was driving a delivery truck for a family who moved into town and tried to start a new cleaning and pressing shop. Hy-Tone Cleaners. Sad thing about this was, that business didn't have a prayer to begin with, and I was part of its failure. Watching that dream die was tough.

Owner's name was Ben. His wife and kid lived in back of the shop, in that old building one block north of the square. Majestic Theater is in the same block. Those people truly lived day-to-day on what the business brought in, and I was the one that brought in the money.

That is, when I delivered the day's cleaning, I was supposed to collect whatever was owed on the work. Few people paid. Sometimes I'd bring back four or five bucks and Ben would be pleased. Sometimes I'd collect almost nothing. Here's a scene that's engraved on my spirit:

About sundown, I drive up to the shop after I've finished my deliveries, and Ben and his wife and child are sitting on the front step, waiting for me, to see how much cash I collected. Whatever it was, Ben would take it across the street to Wolters Grocery and buy food. He'd bring it back and his wife would take it in and fix supper. Sometimes they'd feed me, too.

Those were good people, hard workers, but there just wasn't enough business in town to support that little shop. I still think about them sometimes.

A small cool front has blessed us here at Winedale, along with another half inch of rain.

15 OCTOBER

October came in misbehaving, acting like August, putting us through a streak of 90-degree days. But it has settled down now, and we're getting cool mornings and wonderful blue skies.

I have a poster on my blog who sends word from Amarillo that great flights of sandhill cranes and Canada geese are coming this way. He knows I like to watch for the first flights of these migrants, especially the sandhills. I love the searching calls they send down when they pass over, headed for their winter home on the coastal prairie.

This is Rosie's second birthday. I regret to announce she weighs seventy pounds, about ten more than she should. This is an awful con-dog, able to show signs of fierce hunger when she already has a loaded belly.

Rosie is Babette's dog. She (the dog) won't even come to me when I call her, unless she's convinced I've got a dog biscuit to hand out.

Today, we drove in to Brenham to pick up medicine for all three of us. Yes, that includes the dog. Rosie got bitten, or stung, by something. A big ground hornet, probably.

She's been bitten once by a copperhead and I'm surprised that doesn't happen daily because she roams around looking for dangerous holes to poke her nose in.

And she enjoys going to the vet. All other dogs we've owned hated veterinarians and their hospitals and their pills and needles. Rosie loves them.

20 OCTOBER

Texans are playing the Steelers tonight in Pittsburg. If we had a quarterback we might win. But we haven't had a quarterback since Warren Moon.

The World Series starts tomorrow. Kansas City against the Giants. I was pulling for the Cardinals to go into the Series for the National League, so I'm not much interested in this year's matchup. But I may check in to see how Hunter Pence does in the Series. He's another of the many players that the Astros traded away, and is now doing well. Pence is an outfielder for the Giants. He left Houston behind and ended up in the World Series.

But my favorite baseball player is still Lance Berkman. I like just about everything he does, that I know about. He played first base for the Astros for something like fourteen years. Went to the Yankees as a DH. Then to the Cardinals where he got the hit that won the 2010 World Series. He's retired in Houston now and driving around in a $100,000 automobile but he has driven that car onto the Rice campus and is enrolled to finish getting his degree.

Hear that banging? That's the sound of nail guns on the front porch here at the Winedale place. Our construction project has begun at last. Half the front porch will be closed in to make a new room, and all the back porch will be enclosed, to protect us from the blue northers that make this old house almost unlivable in winter.

When the carpenters began ripping up those old porch floor boards I was there to look underneath, see if I saw a copperhead. I've been convinced for years that families of those snakes make their home beneath this house. Come on, I've seen them crawl out from under there, and go back in when they escaped my long-handled shovel.

No copperheads yet, though. Not even a rat snake. *Bueno.*

Babette has decamped, to office at the library in Round Top. She hates the sound of hammering and sawing. Doesn't bother me. I sort of like it. A friendly noise. Even musical at times. Listen closely and you hear a simple melody in the whine of an electrical saw cutting through a sheet of thick plywood.

On Sunday I got to watch the Texans whip the Tennessee Titans, 30-16, something like that. Texans are 4-4 now at the halfway point of the regular season. I'm betting they'll not be any better than a .500 team after they play eight more games. Beating Tennessee was fun but Tennessee's not much. Haven't won but two games.

Just talked to Becky. She's well. Expecting Mark back from Alabama in November when his golf course reopens.

Water well trouble this morning. Pressure switch on the holding tank is cycling out of control, the needle jumping up to cut-off but immediately falling down to kick-in, up and down, up and down, and this is bad. I can hear those electrical contacts clicking on-and-off, on-and-off, and they're smelling hot and that probably means they're about to burn out.

So, shut the well down and call Harvey's Water Wells, Drilling and Service.

Harvey is dead. He was Harvey Ebert who drilled and maintained hundreds of water wells in this part of the state. His son John and his grandson Jamie carry on the business.

Jamie answers my call. He looks everything over and announces that what you got here, you got a waterlogged system.

I ask Jamie to explain to me how a water well becomes waterlogged. He answers in quick clippy sounds. I think his mouth stays almost closed but I'm not certain because it's hidden way back inside a thick black beard. His little speech sounds something like this to me:

"Well-your-sniffers-scrub-your-check-valve-and-that-gives-you-a-fadeback-on-your-bleeders-and-a-runaway-on-your-recycle-and-you-lose-your-air-pocket-and-that-gives-you-the-waterlog."

He drained the tank and took the pressure switch off and showed me how the contacts were burned black. Put a new switch on and tightened up everything with threads on it. Turned the pump on and waited to see if it kicked in at 30 psi and off at 50, shook my hand and departed. Jamie Ebert, water well mechanic, doing his thing. A citizen of great value to this community.

Out in the country like this, there's no noise more beautiful than the smooth hum of a water well pump.

4 NOVEMBER

Election Day. Babette and I voted early, via U.S. Mail. I voted for Wendy Davis, the pretty woman running for governor, for the Democrats. I would not be comfortable telling you how Babette voted in this race. But you'd have little trouble figuring it out if you followed her on Facebook. Or if you heard her comments at breakfast, when she cusses out the Republicans while reading the political news. My, my. Such startling language, coming out of a nice River Oaks lady, educated in an exclusive college for sophisticated females.

But Babette doesn't need anybody to explain her politics. I better stick to my own.

I was born and raised a Yellow-Dog Democrat. I voted in my first presidential election in '52 and I went for Eisenhower, a Republican, because I thought he'd make a good president and I think he did.

Even when I was still calling myself a Democrat I kept voting in general elections for Republican presidential candidates. With one exception. I voted for Bill Clinton once. I don't remember why, because eventually I was convinced that the Democrats would bankrupt the United States with their spending.

But George Bush and Iraq cured me of voting Republican. And the nasty, evil, racist treatment Republicans have heaped on Obama will probably prevent me from ever casting another Republican vote. I won't live long enough to feel comfortable again calling myself a Republican.

Wendy Davis will get clobbered in today's voting, of course, since Texas hasn't elected a Democrat to a state office in twenty years. But I'm interested in how many votes she gets.

Babette's on a diet and she's been cooking a lot lately. Tonight, salmon in the skillet with rice and that whipped-up spinach dish she makes. If you ask my stomach, life is good.

5 NOVEMBER

The electorate has spoken and it spake Republican, all the way. The Democrats lost control of the U.S. Senate, and the House gained even more Republican clout than it already had. So now the only thing poor Obama can do is sharpen his veto pencil. And encourage those aging Supreme Court justices to eat right and live longer and delay retirement until Hillary comes to the rescue in 2016. Maybe.

Here in Texas Wendy Davis received one-point-eight million votes in the governor's race but Greg Abbott got twice that many. Harris County, loaded with Democrats, voted for Obama in the last general election but went Republican this time. Washington County, where Winedale is, voted Republican eight to one. All ye who enter here, abandon hope.

You want good news? Check the weather. The rain began around nine P.M. Tuesday and it's still coming. Mainly light, and we've measured just two-point-four inches so far. Probably not enough runoff yet to raise water level in our tank, but the forecast is for continued moisture tonight. We're doing better on weather than we did on the election.

7 NOVEMBER

We ended up measuring 3.5 inches from those two days, and most of it soaked in our thirsty ground. I don't believe the tank level rose by any measurable amount.

Our days now are loud with construction noise. The basic frame work on the porch enclosures is done. The carpenters today are nailing in the ceiling, with insulation, of the front porch room. Yesterday was mainly a corrugated tin day. We're using tin for a lot of the exterior walls, giving this old house a sort of hybrid look—a cross, that is, between a house and a barn. I like it. Babette likes it. Rosie likes it. I suspect our neighbors don't like it. They say it's interesting.

This morning I heard my first sandhill crane flight pass over the house. Haven't heard any geese yet.

Comes word now that my old pilot friend Joe Matlock has died, down in Victoria. Joe was one of these rare people who can elevate the quality of your life just by becoming your friend.

He was a pilot for the U.S. Fish and Wildlife Service. For years he flew a high-winged single-engine airplane that the Service used to count the growing population of whooping cranes, down there on the Aransas Wildlife Refuge near Corpus Christi.

I met him in the early '50s, I think it was, when the whooper population was way down, around twenty-five or thirty birds. He was about to make the spring flight to count the cranes. A government wildlife officer was supposed to fly with him but had come down sick and Joe said, "Come on, ride with me."

So, most of that day long, I rode with Joe Matlock at low level, back and forth across that great refuge, like a crop duster, counting whooping cranes on the ground. That was one of the best days of work I ever did, especially since it gained me such a great friend. Joe was an early Texas history buff and later on we did several day's work together, and after dark disposed of a jug or two of Jack Daniel's.

We're about to load up and go to Houston for a few days, mainly for doctor appointments as usual. And for haircuts, and grocery shopping.

In Round Top and Brenham and La Grange we can buy almost

anything in the food line that we need, but meat and fish are the exceptions. On Houston trips we go to Whole Foods and load a cooler with organic chicken and buffalo, which we can't get up here. But mainly we go in for medical reasons.

Babette has been having pain in that left hip joint that was replaced via surgery last spring. Let us pray that she won't have to go through that operation again. Surgery is so hard on her. She's convinced that the anesthesia and the post-op painkiller meds have a lasting negative effect on both her physical and mental health.

I am concerned about the condition of her general health. She is in near-constant pain from arthritis, and no medicine she's tried gives her relief without some damned side effect. She has a bad right knee from years of tennis, and a back problem probably from the same source, and chronic discomfort in her mid-section which bothers me as much as it does her.

But she is losing weight and looking much better in her clothes and that pleases her. Me too.

15 NOVEMBER

We were invited to a sit-down dinner party at the country place of the Graces of Dallas. The Graces are one of the really wealthy families who have a farm in the Round Top area. I thought my wife was the prettiest woman at that dinner. But that's not the first time I ever thought that.

I was a little surprised that we got invited this year. (The Graces throw that party annually.) Because three years ago, the only other time we did attend, I drank maybe two glasses of wine more than I should have, which inspired me to tell my Waxahachie Football Story.

This is an 11 o'clock story and the wine made me tell it at around 8:30 and that was a mistake, even though I did tell it well and it was received with loud laughter and foot stomping. From the men, at least.

I thought one of the Graces at the table disapproved of my story, and sure enough we didn't get invited to the dinner the next year, nor the year after that. So that's why I was surprised that we were invited again this year.

Among the diners was our friend Tom Connor, Houston lawyer who's been a reader of the column for decades. About eight P.M., full of dinner and lots of merlot, Tom got up and reminded the guests that I had attended that dinner before, and had entertained the group with (and I quote here) "his story about the Waxahachie Whore." And he invited me to tell it again.

But I couldn't tell it again. An eleven o'clock story must not be told at eight o'clock. However, I might have relented if it weren't for the fact that Tom had given away the punch line. I was surprised and disappointed in Connor, a man with his experience at drinking wine and attending dinners where stories are told, and there he was messing up my Waxahachie story. His parents in Lamesa raised him better than that.

18 NOVEMBER

Hello from Pirate's Beach on Galveston Island. The hammering and sawing and the coming and going of carpenters at Winedale have finally caused us to run.

We left Rosie at Linda's kennel in Chappell Hill where she was born, and we're in a big four-bedroom beach house about a dozen miles from downtown Galveston.

Babette picked this great house so we could have front-row seats on the beach. The surf at high tide reaches a point not 50 feet from this window I'm looking through just now. The weather is terrible—partly cloudy and cold, and I love it. I've always loved Galveston Island in winter when the summer people are gone and nobody's left but a few pelicans. I can look up and down the beach for more than a mile in either direction and see nothing but sand and surf.

Loafing on the beach is good therapy for me. I never tire of sitting here watching the surf, trying to keep up with the ebb and flow of the tides. I think this steadies my blood pressure. Babette is in yonder working on her stories, or paying bills, or writing letters. She never just does nothing, like I do. Sometimes I wish she would.

I remember a time when I thought the surf, the beach, the whitecaps, everything about the sea, was sad. I was in the Army then, when all the fighting and killing and dying was going on, and there was so much to fear and to grieve.

You know the first time I saw salt water? It was in Newport News, Virginia. We were at a deportation base, to load on troop ships and sail across the Atlantic to Europe where the war was going on. Not a very happy introduction to the ocean.

My outfit boarded a Liberty Ship and many of us stood at the railing on deck and watched the East Coast of the United States fade away, and I know every one of us wondered if we'd ever see it again.

We were twenty-eight days at sea, on the way to Bari, Italy, in the heel of the Italian boot. A nineteen-year-old kid was in a bunk just above me, and he stayed seasick the entire journey. Sometimes he'd vomit in his bunk, and cry for his mother.

I learned to love the seashore, if not the sea itself, when I ended up in Houston after the war and got the column and the delicious freedom to roam, and write about whatever I pleased. A lot of that roaming was along almost 400 miles of Texas coast—beaches and bays and barrier islands and inlets and coves and sandbars and tidal flats and the mouths of half a dozen rivers and square miles of marshland—all of it alive with creatures I'd never known, growing up in West Texas.

Even the *homo sapiens* who populated the Gulf shore were not the same as those in places I knew. They talked different and ate food that I'd never tasted and told good stories that were sometimes true. The stories I loved, and I retold them in my own way in the column.

But the deep blue seas, the oceans way out yonder? They have never converted me. I find them unfriendly. Even boring. Often threatening.

Sure, their depths hide great treasures. And those depths are working alive with swimming animals that feed the planet's population. But they are seldom seen by me, up here above the water.

I've now crossed the Atlantic via ship three times and ridden airliners across it half a dozen trips, and I've seen little to interest me when I look at all that water. The best thing, I've decided, about the surface of the sea is that sooner or later it will touch land. I've said that I love the surf but remember why those waves break and froth and foam to create beauty and entertainment—it's because they have reached the shore.

A few years ago Babette and I flew to New York and got on board Her Majesty's ship the *Queen Mary II* and rode it to London. On that great vessel passengers can watch movies, play games, attend lectures, read bestsellers in libraries, dine in fine restaurants, dance to good band music, gamble in casinos, drink themselves stupid in more bars than I can count.

Maybe you wonder why the ship provides passengers with all those things to do. I will tell you why—it's so they will not die of boredom from looking out portholes at the everlasting ocean.

Our crossing on the Queen Mary took eight days. I remember a voice coming over the PA system on two occasions, calling attention to something of interest.

The first announcement told us that flying fish had been sighted off the starboard bow. They had disappeared, of course, before I could get out on deck for a look. The second announcement informed us that the ship was, at this very moment, passing over the spot where the Titanic went down in 1912. Like everybody else, I hustled to the deck, as if we might see a part of the Titanic sticking out of the water.

I think somebody ought to anchor a large buoy at that spot, with a sign announcing, "The wreck of the Titanic lies 12,600 feet below this buoy." For tourists making this crossing, such a sign would be the main point of interest between New York and London. Everything else—salt water.

It's raining, a little, here on Galveston Island today. Gray clouds floating low. And along comes a flight of eight brown pelicans, soaring an inch above the surf. (Can birds soar that low? Does a soaring bird have to be high? Why?)

Pelicans gliding low this way make a nice demonstration of the efficient use of energy. You just know that they'll crash into the water in the next second if they don't flap a time or two and get a little lift. But they don't flap until long past the time they should, according to the first rule of aerodynamics. How can they do that?

24 NOVEMBER

I'm glad you didn't see us leaving the beach house. It's up on piers, as all houses on Galveston beaches are unless you want a storm tide in your living room. And that means stairs. When we checked in, we hired a guy to lug all our stuff up those stairs.

But we couldn't find him when we checked out, so we had to nurse all our gear down that flight of stairs. Took us hours, coming down one careful step at a time, gripping a suitcase in one hand and clinging to the railing with the other. Not a pretty sight—a ninety-three-year-old man with bad knees, and a seventy-year-old woman with a new hip joint that hadn't healed yet. Where are the Boy Scouts when you need them?

THANKSGIVING DAY

We didn't go anywhere and we didn't have company. We stayed at Winedale and talked about being grateful for our blessings. Babette played with grandson Declan on the computer, via Skype. I spoke to Mark and Becky and they are all right. We had sandwiches. But they were turkey sandwiches instead of chicken, in honor of the occasion.

At night, any night, we watch our shows. We have several we seldom miss. Shows like *Mad Men*, *Madam Secretary*, *The Good Wife*, *Jeopardy*, *The Mentalist*, *Masterpiece*, *Damages*, and others I can't think of now. We record them and usually watch them early in the evening because at nine o'clock we switch off the box and start going to bed, which for some reason now takes three times longer than twenty-five years ago.

CHRISTMAS DAY

We're in Houston to attend the holiday parties we got invited to. Babette went to the beauty shop and had her nails decorated, both finger and toe. She got a haircut, too, which in my opinion she didn't need. If I was in control of her hair it would be flowing down to her behind, the way it was when I met her. She says it's too much trouble to take care of when it's long. I have offered to take care of it myself, but she did not respond to that offer.

What happened at the parties we can't say, since we didn't attend any. This happens to us now and then. We'll go to considerable trouble to get all gussied up for a party, and then decide not to go. We think of something we'd rather do.

I don't enjoy parties the way I once did, mainly because I can't drink any longer, and that's what goes on at the ones we attend. For two hours, everybody stands around in tight groups, sipping and talking.

I have always wondered how such conversational groups are formed. I've tried to form one. Once I stood alone in an ample space, and waited, and waited, but no group formed around me.

I decided I would have to join groups that were already formed and operational, and I did try that but when I walked up to such a group, grinning in a friendly manner, everybody stopped talking. Why? Had they been talking about me?

You understand that BB (Before Babette) I did not associate with these kinds of people. They are much closer to her generation than mine, and almost all are scotch-drinking, tennis-playing, Mercedes-driving, country-clubbing folks who have traveled to every nation in the world except Turkey and they're going there next year.

I don't mean to say they are not good people. They're some of the most civil I've ever met and they've been nice to me. But I've not been able to make a real friend of any of them. Maybe I haven't tried hard enough. I think it would help if I'd ever been to Turkey.

All this Christmas Day we stayed home. Babette cooked a large turkey breast that we'll be eating on for the next four days. We didn't have a Christmas tree but we exchanged modest gifts. Every year, early in December, we decide not to give presents to one another. We make a pact—no gifts, OK? Right, no gifts.

But I often get her something because I know she'll get me something and there I'd be—receiving a gift and having nothing to give.

My favorite system of swapping gifts is when we go to the bookstore. She chooses a couple of books that she really wants and I buy them and give them to her. I pick out a couple of titles that I like and she buys them and gives them to me. That way we're sure to get a book that we really want, and we don't have to wrap them.

This doesn't work with children. Children need surprises at Christmas.

30 DECEMBER

Sad news. Jack Loftis, the *Chronicle* editor who hired me when I left the *Post* and went over to the *Chronicle*, has died. He was 80. We'll be going in for his memorial service Jan. 7. Jack was a truly good human.

One of the best phone calls I ever received came from him. I was sitting in the *Post* newsroom one afternoon in 1984, not really in high spirits. The Hobbys had sold the paper to that bunch of Canadians who had made some changes that didn't please me, and I was actually thinking of quitting.

Thinking of it, yeah, but where would I go? What would I do? I'd been at the *Post* thirty-two years. It was the only newspaper I'd ever worked for. Almost the only newspaper I'd ever been in.

Mary Rolon, the newsroom receptionist, hollered at me, said I had a call on her line. Which surprised me because I seldom got calls at the paper. I always worked at home, took my stuff in, or sent it. I didn't even have a desk or a telephone at the *Post*.

I'd never met Jack Loftis. He was assistant editor of the *Chronicle* then. That day he made one of the shortest calls of its kind in communication history. He said the *Chronicle* wanted to hire me and would I be interested in having lunch to talk about it. I said yes and he said how about noon tomorrow at the Confederate House and I said fine.

At lunch I guess we talked about money but I don't remember it. I went over to the Cronk for about twice what the Canadians were paying me. I waited a couple of years before I confessed to Loftis that I had grown unhappy at the *Post* and he could have had me for a lot less.

2015

NEW YEAR'S DAY

We did try. On New Year's Eve we stayed up and watched an extra show and didn't get to bed until almost 11 o'clock.

I was about to quit reading and turn off my light when our across-the-creek neighbor Randon Dillingham set off a fireworks display. He is 60-something years old but hasn't yet outgrown the need to make great noises at New Year's.

2 JANUARY

Our year is off to a sour start. The phone brought us more sad news, when we hadn't yet recovered from the first. Babette's sister-in-law, Kathy Fraser, called about the death of her husband, Ken. I've never been able to remember Ken's last name. He was Kathy's second husband and a nice fellow, a retired geologist.

Kathy's first husband was Wilson Fraser, Babette's half-brother. There's my connection to Kathy and her husbands. All these folks are intelligent, handsome people. Via her first husband, Kathy has a beautiful family. My favorite of the bunch is Bill Fraser, a super-sharp fellow who was really helpful to Babette when the management of her family corporation was dumped in her lap a few years back.

Kathy herself is a special person, a gin-drinking Episcopalian who will lecture you about religion with a Bible in one hand and a martini in the other.

Tomorrow is daughter Becky's birthday. She must be 60 or more by now.

Enchiladas for supper, from Los Patrones in Round Top. On a scale of 10 I give them about a 6.

8 JANUARY

We've made our monthly trip to Houston, this time to attend Jack Loftis' funeral. Which I thought was a curious service. (I've lately become interested in funerals.)

It was held in a funeral home, not a church, and that was appropriate because there was nothing religious about this service. Jack was a serious fan of bluegrass, and a bluegrass band came in and played either quietly or too-loudly, from start to quit.

Three people made speeches. Tony Pederson, former managing editor of the *Chronicle*. Then a nervous Loftis family member who made the audience uncomfortable with his suffering. I forget his name. Then *Chronicle* columnist Ken Hoffman, a neighbor and close personal friend to Jack.

Most of the males in the crowd, even the Chronk's reporters, had on their dark suits and neckties but Hoffman wore khaki pants and what looked like a wrinkled wind-breaker, no tie. He told funny stories about his association with Loftis.

A fourth guy who never gave his name served as emcee. He told a joke that was a little off-color and had nothing whatever to do with Jack Loftis or a funeral or anything else appropriate to the event.

Maybe he just wanted to get a laugh because throughout the service the crowd did laugh a great deal, and they clapped a lot, too. They clapped when the band played, and when the speakers finished speaking. Even when that guy told the bad joke, they clapped and clapped.

After the service I visited with my former copy editor, Betty Luman. She thought all that applause was curious at a funeral but said clapping is apparently growing more common everywhere, even in some churches when the choir sings, and when the preacher concludes his sermon.

I was on the back row and I didn't see a tear shed at this funeral. To me, that's good. When people have had their lives, been here long enough to do whatever they do, there's no point in wailing and moaning in deep grief over them. That just makes everybody feel terrible. I once quit going to funerals, for years, on account of this.

A child's death, though, there's something to grieve about. Or any young person. I can still feel pain, after seventy years, when I think of the guys I knew during WWII, guys twenty-one and twenty-two years old who died in combat.

I think about Herbert Flowers, one of the best humans ever to walk on this planet. I knew him in college, at Texas Tech. A good old grinning country boy who loved life. Intelligent. Wise. Mature. There in Lubbock he'd met a pretty girl and they were exactly right for one another. They were just sick in love. They'd huddle in the library and plan their lives.

And then Herbert had to go overseas and die in the tail gunner's turret of a B-17.

I just now read over what I wrote about Jack Loftis' funeral and it sounds critical, but I didn't intend that. I've written a sort of procedure I'd like followed at my own funeral, and I expect many would consider it pretty strange, and maybe stranger than anything that went on at Jack's service.

What I don't want is sad organ music and a go-to-hell sermon. I've always thought that, instead, I'd like to give a little talk at my service. I could do that by making a recording, but I've always hated the sound of my voice on a recorder.

So I've written the speech and my friend Steve Smith, retired anchor of Houston Channel 11, has agreed to show up and read it if he's still alive at the time. Steve has this strong beautiful voice, and he's a pro reader, and I think this would be nice. My words, in Steve's voice.

Then also I have a commitment from David Horsley of Amarillo to deliver a sermonette. David is a preacher/carpenter/newspaper columnist/book author and my long-time friend.

And I want music on records by Willie and Merle and anything else Babette night want to throw in.

The trouble with a plan like this, the funeral has got to happen pretty soon, or it won't fly. If I happened to fool around and live another five years, or even three, by then I'll have been pretty well forgotten and nobody would show up. I've told Babette, if she thinks I can't draw a crowd, I want her to junk my plan and use her own, whatever she wants.

Another weakness of my plan is that David or Steve might mess up and die before I do. I've told them both that they're not allowed to do any such thing, but neither is much good about taking orders. I check on them now and then, to see how they're feeling.

15 JANUARY

We're having a pretty good string of cold days here at Winedale. Not much freezing but several lows into the 30s, along with frequent drizzle. The drizzle is what we need, so the soil will get soaked and save the trees that were weakened during the last two years of drouth. We have five mature live oaks inside the yard fence and two of them are showing unhappy symptoms.

The tank is full now, and Rosie swims in it daily, even on the coldest days. All the fish I stocked last spring are gone, dead during the dry summer. I doubt I'll try to replace them. I've about had enough of fishing.

A few summers ago our friends Christy and Bill Manuel invited us to spend a week on an island Christy's family owns in Lake Huron. I packed a fly rod up there, just so I could say I fished in that Great Lake, and I caught a four-pound smallmouth bass. I let him go. Told him he was the last fish I'd ever catch, and thanked him very much.

But he wasn't the last. Not long afterward I was visiting Mark and Becky, who have lived close to the Gulf for years and become salt-water fisherfolk. When they were little I taught both of them how to dig for worms and bait a hook and rig a line and fish in rivers and lakes, but I've never learned to fish in salt water. They took me way out on Texas City Dike and rigged a popping-cork above a live shrimp and Mark cast it out halfway to Africa and I caught a beautiful big speckled trout. We brought it home and Mark cleaned it and Becky cooked it some special way and this was a sweet experience. That night I lay in bed a long time thinking about it, and about a lot of other things, and I cried.

17 JANUARY

A crispy Saturday afternoon at Winedale. I just now scattered a quart of black-oil sunflower seed for the birds in the back yard and we have cardinals and doves and chickadees and woodpeckers and little song sparrows and even a few big old fat crows, out there eating. I need to put out more seed.

We're about to load up tomorrow and go back to Houston for a week, to escape the painters. Our construction project— enclosing sections of the front and back porch to give us two more rooms—is in the painting stage. We run from paint. Babette is dangerously sensitive to the fumes and they're a threat to me because I can't smell them.

I can't, in fact, smell anything now. I remember Maifred[1] making that same announcement when she was nearing 90. "I have lost my sense of smell." I wonder if the same thing has happened to IR[2].

Also I wonder how close I'd need to get to a skunk before I began smelling him. But I don't need to find that out.

26 JANUARY

We're back from spending the week in Houston. Babette went to the beauty salon and I got a haircut, about two weeks after I needed one. Carol the Barber, who has been shearing my locks for thirty years and parting my hair on the left side, suddenly decided that it ought to be parted on the right.

It does not like to be parted on the right, and looks really bad. I got out of her barber chair and drove straight to the apartment and tried to shampoo that punk haircut off my head. But it didn't work. I have been cold ever since on my right side because Carol cut away so much covering that's been protecting my head, I guess since my first haircut.

I don't know why people can't leave alone things that don't need to be changed.

Babette has been trying to steer me to a hair stylist and a manicurist and a pedicurist. But I don't want anybody messing with my toes, poking sharp instruments under their nails. And I would feel unfaithful, letting anybody other than Carol the Barber cut my hair. She depends on the income, so I will go back to her in another month, except next time I'm making an advance speech

1. Maifred Hale Cullen, Hale's oldest sister
2. Ima Ruth Taylor, Hale's other sister, also older

about my hair and how it likes to be parted on the left side. It suits my politics.

Terry the skilled cabinet maker is here today, to put handles on our new screen doors. He is serving as general contractor on this construction job. Our agreement says that all the work was to be finished by December 31. It was not. I think it will be finished by the middle of February, but I can't say February of what year.

Never mind, Terry is a nice fellow and does pretty work. He is almost finished with the front porch enclosure which will become my office, according to Babette. Being retired, I didn't know I needed an office, but it looks nice and I like it. It'll make me a good bear's nest.

This old country house is home now. We've even started calling it home. We used to sit on the front porch here and talk about things we needed to do at home, meaning Houston. Now when we're in Houston we talk about things that need doing at home, meaning Winedale.

If I could afford it I would tell Terry to stick around another year and build Babette a modern kitchen. The kitchen is all right but it's in fierce need of more work space. And it doesn't have a garbage disposal, so we're still emptying leftover mashed potatoes into a plastic garbage bag and carrying it out. I'm glad Babette's mother doesn't know that her daughter, reared in swanky River Oaks and educated at Sweet Briar and London School of Economics, is living in an old farm house without a garbage grinder.

But she does have a garbage carrier-outer, who works cheap and doesn't roam around after dark.

Talking about offices, the best place I ever had to work was the room we built on the back of Babette's house not long after we married, or maybe it was just before.

The worst place I ever had was at *The Houston Post*, in the old Post building on the southwest corner of the Polk and Dowling intersection. Went to work there in the fall of 1947. That building is gone now.

They gave me a little desk about two and a half feet wide, up against the back wall of the newsroom. Just the other side of that wall was a bank of about a dozen teletype machines that rocked and rolled and made their shattery, clattery racket most of every day and night.

In summer I kept a little drugstore thermometer on my desk and it would often climb to 90 degrees. AC? No, not in that building. It had wide hinged windows on the east side and they let fresh air in if the wind was right. But none of that freshness ever reached my desk.

Some good things happened to me in that dreary corner, and a few bad ones, too. The worst of them was something my first wife, Helen, did.

We had been married I guess a couple of years when she decided that I was fooling around on her, seeing other women. I was doing no such thing, but Helen could see marriage trouble in almost anything I did. At home if I got a phone call from a woman at the paper, say an editor on the copy desk, Helen was certain the call was from somebody I was seeing on the sly. She was so jealous. It was a sickness with her.

I was carrying a Speed Graphic camera then, developing negatives and printing my own pictures, and one afternoon late I had to go in to the paper and soup my negs, get prints ready for my Sunday page. Helen rode along with me. Mimi, her mother, must have been visiting us then, and stayed home with the baby, I'm not sure.

Anyway, when I stopped in the *Post* parking lot, Helen decided to go in with me. Said she'd never seen where I worked.

I guided her to my desk and got her seated in my chair where she could wait for me. The newsroom was full of people, working.

When I got back, after maybe half an hour, she had pulled out every drawer of my desk and was reading letters I'd saved, all having to do with my work, like story ideas that readers sent in. Obviously she thought she'd find letters from all those women I was supposed to be chasing. It was just so obvious, to all my co-workers, what she was doing.

She found nothing, of course, but the scene was a deep embarrassment to me. I felt it damaged me, professionally. Afterward, Helen and I stayed married for twenty years, until the kids were grown and gone. But my feeling for her was never really the same after that day.

I think I could have forgiven her if she'd asked for it. She never did. It wasn't in her to say she was sorry.

But I better add this: Later, before that marriage was all over, I had committed a few trespasses of my own. I did say I was sorry for them and eventually Helen and I were able to talk as friends, sort of, but I don't remember that she ever forgave me. She's gone now and I'm calling it even.

Well, I was talking about places to work.

I loved what we built on the back of Babette's house. It was somewhat like a studio apartment, with a big U-shaped desk and book cases and a nice bath with a huge tub that had those nozzles—what do you call those things? There was a bed for naps and for making love on rainy afternoons and a little refrigerator and a cooktop with two burners and lots and lots of wall space for calendars and clippings and pictures and do-dads you don't want to throw away quite yet.

I grieve to write that this is all gone now. Levelled by a bulldozer, and the house with it, and a new blocky 10-room box built on the lot. We never should have left that place.

Been another pretty winter day in Washington County. Santa Fe sky. Gentle breeze. High of 74. This a Tuesday, so it's fried chicken night at J.W's restaurant, eight miles away in Carmine.

29 JANUARY

Started moving books and a few pieces of furniture into the new rooms formed by the porch enclosures. Gonna be nice. The glass outside walls work great. You'd think you were sitting outdoors, except next summer when the temp gets wicked high, we'll have cool air out there.

I dreamed last night that I was lost in a strange city in Indonesia. I wonder why. In all my ninety-three years I've not spent five minutes thinking of Indonesia and here I am dreaming about it. Babette asked how I knew I was in Indonesia. I knew because I met a fellow and asked him where I was and he said, "Indonesia." I need to look on a map and find out exactly where I went.

Babette reads the astrology charts every morning. She is a Cancer. She tells me she doesn't take the information too seriously but I believe it's an influence in her decisions. That is, if she packed a bag to go to Austin for one night, and her horoscope told her she should not travel today, I think she would change plans and stay home, maybe.

Me, I'm a Gemini. I seldom read what the stars have in store for Geminis because I forget to look, but Babette sometimes tells me what my horoscope says, especially if it's something positive. My suspicion is that if it's negative, she doesn't mention it.

I don't discount everything about astrology, because I know practically nothing about it. And the years have taught me it's not wise to reject a concept simply because I don't understand it.

Who knows what influence the heavenly bodies have on a puny little old planet like ours? Here's the moon, just about the least complex heavenly body we know anything about, and it influences the tides of our oceans. Now, to accept that the stars affect the daily lives of individuals on Earth, that's a mighty long reach for me.

Even so, you can find people who believe that the stars had a huge influence on the affairs of this nation, back when Reagan was dozing through his last term in office. And Nancy was running the country with her favorite astrologist.

No, I just said you can find people who believe that.

31 JANUARY

The last day of the new year's first month, and a pretty nice day, too. Babette is cooking a whole chicken in a great big pot, with lots of onion and later on will come carrots and celery and potatoes and a variety of spices. Even I can smell this and I'm not close to the kitchen.

She'll take the meat off that bird when it's done, and let the juice, with all the bones, cook way down. To make stock. We have this as soup and it's powerful good stuff, with little pieces of bread dropped in. And the meat is so tender and sweet and makes wonderful sandwiches for two or three days.

Talked to Ima Ruthie a couple of days ago. She sounds ancient on the phone—well, who doesn't, at ninety-six—but says she is not in pain, that they take care of her well, that she couldn't talk long because she was about to watch the Dallas Mavericks play Memphis and the game was fixing to start.

Have I mentioned my new hobby? What it is, it's thinking up ways to rescue words that I've known for eighty-something years, but have forgotten. Doctor tells me losing words that way is standard for people my age but it truly irritates me.

These are not difficult words, and I have managed to get a few of them back via mnemonics. There, that's my trouble. I can remember mnemonic, a difficult word if I ever met one, but it is always available to me. And yet I had lost, for example, the word migraine.

I have migraine symptoms frequently (without the awful headaches, thank heaven) and it's a term I need. When I have my eyes examined for new glasses, I need to talk to the doctor about migraine. So I have dreamed up a mnemonic for the word. I think of a field of mature grain. It's wheat, I think. So when I need migraine and it won't come, I call up my field of grain and it moves me right on to migraine.

Strange, I know. You'd think remembering migraine would be harder than calling up a field of wheat, and for other people I'm sure it is, but not for me.

Proper names have become truly difficult. I met Rigby Owen in Round Top this morning. I have known Rigby for I guess sixty years. He was editor and publisher of the *Conroe Courier*, and a stringer for the *Post*, and I couldn't remember his name. But I can't afford to invest the effort it takes to create a trick to remember the names of people, even friends like Rigby. The proper names I work to remember are mostly those of businesses, important in the conduct of daily affairs.

An example is Walgreen's, the drug chain. A few years ago the name Walgreen's left me, and I missed it something awful because we get meds there and obviously I need that name.

I got it back, thanks to a concrete wall that juts up just behind the Walgreen's drugstore in Brenham. When I need the name of that store, I visualize that wall, and those four letters are always enough to bring up the green and complete the name I need.

Some words simply refuse to return to me, once I've lost them. One is the family name of the native trees that grow on the mountains near Santa Fe. No, not aspen. Not cedar. Not pine.

Only way I've ever figured out how to get it to reveal itself is to pass down the alphabet until I come to the first letter in the name. A,b,c,d,e,f,g,h,i,j—*juniper*! There it is. But it'll be gone again in the next five minutes. And sometimes even this system won't work, so when I arrive at j, instead of juniper I get jasmine, or jeopardy, or jingle.

Thought for the day: Love is not having to say "bless you" every time your spouse sneezes. We do a fat lot of sneezing around here.

2 FEBRUARY

Ground Hog Day. The weather has gone wintry again, cold and wet and yet not wet enough to do much good.

I'm told we don't have ground hogs in Texas. If we did have one, and if he came out of his hole today, he wouldn't have seen his or any other shadow. I think we ought to import a few of the creatures. Make February a little more interesting.

5 FEBRUARY

Went into town (Round Top) yesterday and paid the January bill at R.T. Mercantile. I like to pay it in person. Hand the check to Jackie—$349.38 this time—and watch her grin.

Our favorite Round Top merchants may be Debbie and Gerald Tobola at The Copper Shade Tree. This is a shop that offers arty objects created by people who live in such places as Muldoon and Raccoon Bend. The Shade Tree also sells books, including world-famous titles such as *Bonney's Place* and *Paper Hero*. If every book store in Texas had sold as many of my books as Debbie and Gerald, I would be grinning like Jackie at Mercantile.

Yesterday a tall, attractive woman named Jancy Ervin came here to the house. She is an interior designer from Brenham. Rosie rushed in and began sniffing her, showing total approval, and Jancy remarked as so many visitors do, "She's probably smelling my dog."

I wonder if all dog owners go around giving off the same odors their dogs do. So that you have people smelling like greyhounds, and bulldogs, and poodles, and St. Bernards.

Jancy Ervin was here to consult with Babette about what we might do to make this old house nicer, at least on its inside. I doubt there's much more to be done about its outside, covered as it is mostly with corrugated tin so that its appearance suggests both a house and a barn. Maybe we should call it a bouse. Or a harn?

I still haven't heard what this designer thought about our interior. I could hear her say, "I like that." Or sometimes, "That's interesting." I do know what the latter remark means. It means, "Well, everybody to his own taste, as the old woman said when she kissed the cow."

Tamales for supper, bought at the organic farmers market in Brenham. Not bad. I gave 'em a seven. I now judge all tamales against those made by Rosaria, the faithful *esposa* of Vicente Borrego, native of the Mexican State of Tamalipas and now a taxpaying citizen of Brazoria County, Texas. Old Friend Morgan and

I used to take a couple of dozen of Rosaria's tamales on our trip south to meet spring. When we met it, we'd pull off the road and build a fire and heat the tamales in foil and I always called them tens, whether they were or not. Even cold they were eights.

6 FEBRUARY

In Scotty's Restaurant in Round Top I was nursing a mug of coffee, waiting on a take-out order, and this young fellow wearing hunting camos sat down and we talked. About the weather, about barbecue, about military service. He was about to go into the Army.

He said, "You never wrote about your combat experience. How come?"

I used to get that question a lot. Actually I always thought I wrote what was appropriate to tell, about my experience in that war. And now a library half full of books about WWII combat has been written, and almost all of it more interesting than mine. Over there in Italy in '44 and '45, in the 15th Air Force, we got up before dawn and loaded onto B-24's and flew across the Adriatic and dropped bombs on places like Munich and Vienna and came home and ate supper and hit the sack and got up the next morning and did it again.

We got shot at, sure, by German anti-aircraft units and our bomber would get hit, by chunks of flak, on every mission. But they were mainly small hits, in our case. Other crews weren't so lucky.

In my customary spot in the top turret, I saw as much combat as I care ever to see. I've looked ahead when we were on a bomb run, about to pass over a target, and seen a B-24 take a direct flak hit and go spiraling down, with ten guys aboard. At night you told yourself, Well, sure, that could happen to us tomorrow, but the odds are that it won't.

It almost did, however, time and again. When you survive a tour of combat missions, you're going to have close calls.

My own closest call happened in December of '44, on a mission deep into Germany, starting from down in the heel of the Italian boot. I've written about this, I think in the book "Paper Hero," but not in great detail. Over the years, though, the story becomes more and more significant to me personally, and I think about it far more often now than I did in the year after it happened.

On that mission I was not flying with my regular crew. I had checked out as a radar jammer, and jammers flew only on bombers equipped with the jammer units. These units were designed to interfere with radar the enemy used to track attacking bombers and aim their anti-aircraft guns.

So I was sitting on the left side of the flight deck, just behind the pilot, when an 88-millimeter shell struck our bomber on its right wing, near the fuselage, between the fuselage and the Number 3 engine.

Now hear this: The shell did not detonate.

It passed through the wing, leaving a hole almost perfectly round. It had slightly ragged edges. Its diameter—I'm guessing now—was approximately seven inches.

I have since gone to bed many nights with this thought lingering in my head: I have had another day of life, only because an 88 mm shell failed to explode over Germany in 1944.

I have never shared that thought with anyone. I've never written the details of that mission because they are not about what happened, but about what did not. It is my own personal war horror story.

Those of us in the B-24's accepted the popular notion that the Germans were the best anti-aircraft shooters on the planet. They had splendid guns and their gunners were damn well trained and they got better and better in late '44 and early '45 as the war moved toward its end. Most of those weapons were mobile. Late in the conflict a group of bombers moving on Munich, for example, or Vienna, could be facing flak from a concentration of as many as 250 guns.

At mission briefings, the announcement of that many guns at the target always generated moans and groans from the crews. (I went to Vienna six times and Munich twice.)

On a mission of this kind, information about altitude was considered vital, by both sides. The Germans armed their ack-ack ammo to detonate at specific elevations. So those of us in the bombers never mentioned our correct altitude when we talked on radio between planes. Each mission had a prearranged "base altitude," like 18,000 feet. If our true altitude was 22,000 feet and we needed to mention it, we'd call it "base plus four."

Whether this really fooled the enemy I don't know. I doubt it. I also doubt that those of us flying radar jammers ever jammed any radar. The Germans always seemed to know how high we were, what target we were headed for, and sometimes even the name of the officer flying the lead plane of a given group.

We were flying that day with a crew of eleven. I have decided that if the shell had detonated, two of the eleven might have been lucky enough to survive.

I've never been able to figure a way that the eight men in the front of the airplane could have gotten out. These were the pilot and copilot. Bombardier. Navigator. Nose gunner. Engineer. Radar jammer. Radio operator/Top turret gunner. (In our outfit, over enemy territory the radio operator left his position and manned the top turret. On an ordinary mission, that would be me).

Parachutes? Sure, every man was equipped with a chute, which was useless if he's trapped inside a falling bomber. A B-24 with a wing shot off will travel one direction and that's down. Maybe in a steep dive, maybe in a flat spin. These guys would try to get out, provided they were conscious, but I'm giving them little chance.

This leaves three crew members, toward the rear of the plane. The tail gunner, waist gunner and ball turret gunner.

Even though his position is farthest from the center of the explosion, I can't see the tail gunner surviving because he needs to crawl out of his turret and make his way to a waist window to bail out. He'll never make it. Heaven knows what kind of gyrations the tail section of the bomber is going through, on its way down.

So now we have the two remaining gunners to account for. I've always felt that if any of us survived, these two might get out of the airplane alive. When the shell hit, the waist gunner would be standing at the large open waist window with his parachute on, and he might get out. Be thrown out, maybe.

I think the belly man might also have managed an exit because we had not seen any fighters that day. I know sometimes when there were no fighters and a lot of flak, the belly man would raise his turret and get out, when we went over a target. He might have gone through one of the waist windows.

Even assuming that both those guys opened their chutes, what awaited them on the ground probably wasn't a lot better than what happened to the others of us.

Well, a reader might consider that this is a mighty detailed report about an event that never happened. But it did happen. Not to my crew, but to many others.

What really happened to us that day doesn't make a chilling war story but it was a pretty serious adventure. Here's how I remember it:

When the 88 went through the right wing, our bomber fell into a steep bank and slid out of formation and seemed, to me, to be out of the pilot's control. There was a lot of talking and yelling on the intercom until we gradually leveled out. Finally somebody called for an oxygen check and every position checked in OK. I stood and looked into the cockpit and the pilot was holding his yoke 90 degrees off the position it should have been for level flight. So obviously some of the control cables had been severed. Not a happy condition when you're four hours from home over enemy territory.

The pilot, his voice somewhat shaky, announced he wasn't sure how long he could keep control, that the crew should prepare to bail out. But don't jump until he gave the word.

I looked down. Exactly where we were I don't know but the view below was not inviting. We were over mountains, their peaks capped with snow. Bailing out over those peaks? Not a pleasant prospect.

So we waited, intercoms silent. When the pilot spoke again he sounded better. He made us a little speech. Understand this is a man probably twenty-five years old. (I was twenty-three at the time and the eldest of the non-coms on my regular crew.)

He gave us an option. He wanted to try to fly home but he wasn't certain he could control the bomber in a turn, at least not a steep bank like he'd need in a landing pattern. But he was doing pretty well flying level. When we got into friendly radio contact, he'd try to find one of our bases on the Italian coast that would clear him for a long shallow approach.

He wasn't guaranteeing he could land that thing but he wanted to try. The option was, we could ride on in with him, or bail out now.

This kind of speech was probably already common in war movies none of us had yet seen. But it was new to me and I was impressed. I looked down at those mountain peaks one more time and voted to stay aboard. So did everybody else.

It was a long, slow ride back across the Adriatic, gradually losing altitude. Radio communication was set up at a friendly strip maybe 200 miles from our home base. Making one of the longest final approaches in the history of aviation, that pilot skinned the B-24 in slick as milk. We all piled out, laughing and clapping one another on the back like a bunch of college kids who'd just won a football game. Then we gathered beneath the right wing and took turns looking up through the hole, made by the shell that didn't explode.

For three or four days we loafed at that base, shooting baskets in the gym and reading dog-eared paperbacks in the day room. Then we all rode back home in the bed of a GI truck. And flew another mission the next day.

24 FEBRUARY

Back to ordinary daily doings in the country. Here is my Winedale routine, sort of:

After I let Rosie out and make coffee, I switch on my computer and check e-mail and the blog to see if anybody has written me while I slept. This is mainly a habit of the years when I was writing the column and getting reaction from the readers. What I get now is mostly spam, except when the posters on the blog get stirred up about something. Then I'll have a flock of comments, to read and either publish or delete.

With my second cup of coffee I check the biggest and blackest headlines on the *Chronicle* and the *New York Times* (their online editions, since we can't get delivery out here among the coyotes and the hoot owls.)

If there's nothing I need to read right now, I fix my usual summer breakfast—shredded wheat with red grapes and soy milk—

and return to the newspapers. I have finally learned to read a newspaper on a computer while eating breakfast, without dripping milk onto the keyboard.

I'd much rather have the print editions, even though opening the pages makes me sneeze. Paper dust.

Around seven-thirty I feed the dog and by eight o'clock Babette is up and drinking her Earl Grey tea and speaking in baby talk to Rosie. If I have read something in the papers that she will consider good news, I go ahead and tell her about it while she's drinking tea. If it's something she'll consider really rotten news, I don't tell her about it yet because it'll get her day started off wrong. She'll hear about it soon enough.

When the time is right, we swap dreams. That is, we tell one another what we dreamed about during the night. I enjoy this. Me, I'm a streak dreamer who may go dreamless for weeks but Babette is a major league dreamer. She dreams every night. And her dreams are complex and entertaining. I suspect she often has dreams she doesn't tell me about but that's all right, a dream is highly personal and may not be suitable for sharing.

Next, I clean up the kitchen, according to an agreement of long standing.

Washing dishes is not my favorite activity and making up beds is a true pain in the ass. But if you knew the details of this agreement, you would understand that it's a sweet deal for me.

Taking my old-man pills is next. One for my blood pressure, one for my prostate, and three vitamins—a multiple, a B-12 and a D-3. I wonder how many years I've taken these pills, making handsome profits for the pharmaceutical industry. (How in the unshirted hell do you spell pharmasootical?)

I like to imagine that somewhere there's a poor struggling druggist with a sick wife who needs expensive surgery and she says to her husband, "Honey, how will we ever pay for this costly operation?" and her husband replies, "Don't worry, dear, we'll be fine just as long as Hale's blood pressure stays high and his prostate keeps enlarging."

7 MARCH

Check the date immediately above. I haven't written a sentence on the journal since the 24th of February. Reason is, I've put all routine activity on hold and I'm trying to write a screenplay (or parts of one) based on my old Christmas of 1930 story, about living on the sheep ranch near Granbury.

Due to the frightening collapse of crude oil prices (from more than $100 a barrel to below forty-five, we've decided that we better start making a little money instead of spending so much of it. I think this screenplay idea is a long shot at a moving target but we're into it as if we know what we're doing.

Plan is that Babette writes an outline and I come along and provide dialogue where needed and then Babette builds a finished screenplay of maybe a hundred pages. Which we'll then sell for whatever we can get.

Today I have no idea that what I'm writing on the screenplay will be any good, or even whether it's suited to the goal we've set. But stay tuned.

This has been a hell of a hard winter for the Midwest and the East with record snowfalls and wicked blizzards. Here at Winedale we've had plenty of cool weather and two or three light freezes but not a lot of rain. Due to many solid cloudy days of high humidity the countryside is looking green and promising. But I'd like to see some rain, so we can go into summer with moist topsoil and full stock tanks.

For lunch today we had tamales from the Brenham store specializing in local and organic products. Not bad, considering they were frozen, and somewhat dry when thawed out in the micro-wave. A little dab of Tabasco didn't hurt.

While we ate I told Babette about the first tamales I ever ate, on Bewick Street in Ft. Worth when I was in second grade. I remember my father getting out of our old car on a cold, cold night, to buy tamales from an ancient Hispanic man standing beside a two-wheeled cart near the T&P Railroad tracks. Ten cents a dozen. The tamales were heated in a large metal can in the bed of the cart. When the lid came off that can, steam billowed into the wind.

We went home and ate those tamales with saltine crackers and ketchup.

8 MARCH

Half inch of rain during the night, and I forgot to spring the kitchen clock forward an hour, so we can live in Daylight Saving Time.

Today we must gather up and get ready to go to Houston, where Babette has a book club meeting and we both have appointments with the doctor. And I have a date with Carol the Barber for an over-due haircut.

Rosie goes to the kennel while we're gone. I'm looking forward to her kennel visit because that dog is really tired of me. I hope they can take a couple of pounds off her, since she has stopped growing up and instead is growing out, in all directions.

18 MARCH

As you see by the above dateline, I haven't been doing much jour-naling lately. We survived that week in Houston and I got a good report from my doctor after a flock of annual tests. Doctor says I was standing in the right line when they handed out the genes, so I always get nice readings on my blood work.

But that doesn't do much for the old ticker. My EKG showed that my heart is still in active fibrillation, without much prospect that it'll ever calm down and take up a regular beat. I walk around here at Winedale weak as a Baptist cocktail. There is no strength left in me anywhere. That's why, for the last few years, I'm always a little surprised when I wake up in the morning.

I tell that to friends and they say, "Well, dying in your sleep would be a nice way to go." Maybe so but if I'm given a choice, I'd choose another way. I'd sort of like to know that I'm going.

I know, being awake and dying at the same time seems an inconsistent condition but I have been in it a time or two (or thought I was) and I didn't mind it.

One morning a couple of years ago I was walking, or trying to walk, down a long hall that led to the emergency room in Houston's Methodist Hospital. I was suffering, as I later learned, from a super-critical case of dehydration and anemia, in addition to all my other infirmities.[3]

I felt that every halting step would be the last before I fell. I still believe that the only reason I ever arrived at the ER is that I kept reaching forward, searching for a handle to grab onto so I could stay up, and pull myself along. Of course, no such handle existed. I was clawing along a slick bare wall.

When they got me into a room I managed to produce an extraordinary volume of blood, dark purple in color. Somebody then got me into a bed, and I sunk into pure peace. No pain. No worry. No concern about anything. And I thought, Hey, this is it, I'm dying, and it's beautiful.

Next thing I remember, a guy was sticking a needle into my arm, for a blood transfusion.

---

3. The result of a blood-thinning medication called Pradaxa.

23 MARCH

We have a chamber-of-commerce Monday here at Winedale. Baby blue skies and a mild breeze and lots of bird activity. We have a few bluebonnets blooming in the back yard and a lot of paintbrush near the bloom stage.

But I'm on a guilt trip this morning, about not driving out to Goldthwaite for Belton Hightower's funeral a few days ago. If I had died he would have come to my service, if the strength to do it was still in him.

Old Belton was a faithful friend. He did more dreaming then I ever did about *Bonney's Place* becoming a movie. This was a life's goal to him, and he did a lot to keep the story a viable film property. He stirred up the money to buy the rights. Got on the phone in his tack shop and talked to the actor Ben Johnson, and got him interested in the story, and Johnson's estate still owns the *Bonney* film rights at this date.

Belton helped me get out of Pasadena[4] when I needed out of there desperately. Gave me a place to stay temporarily, and told benevolent lies on the phone about where I was, at a time when I didn't want to be found.

Thinking about Belton has brought up the memory of other close friends I want to include in this journal, this record, this whatever-it-is. Some have already been mentioned. Most are dead, but not all.

Going all the way back to Eastland and my early youth, the best boyhood friend I ever had was Guy (Dude) Wilkins. We practically lived together, hunted and fished together, roamed the woods and fields together, for several years of our growing-up time. I've told some of this, and will no doubt tell more.

---

4. A difficult situation at the end of his second marriage.

Dude was (is) a year older than I, and at this very hour is probably playing golf out there in Utah. Once or twice a year he checks
in to my Facebook, to see if I'm still alive.

(Small airplane just flew over the house, very low altitude,
almost like a buzz, so I went out to see if it was going to come
back. It didn't. I used to have pilot friends who could have buzzed
us. Joe Matlock. Bill Shearer. But they're both dead.

Here at Winedale we have a pilot neighbor, Tommy Jacomini,
who once buzzed the house when Babette and her dog were out
in the yard. That was the day I was riding with him, in his pretty
little bright yellow tail-dragger.)

Most of the pals of my early times were music friends who
played in the high school band with me, and in the dance band
started by Jack Brown. These were E.J. Pryor, Jim and Bob
Galloway, Pat Owen, Leo Wolf.

Leo taught me to drive, in his parents' 1938 Chrysler with its
fluid drive transmission. When I was needing to learn how, Fred
Hale would be gone for weeks at a stretch in his old Chevy with
its worn-out clutch. So our family was mainly carless. We walked
everywhere. If a destination was too far to walk, we didn't go.

Sister Maifred, not yet twenty-one, was supporting the family.
No matter what the weather—103 heat, twenty degrees cold,
rain, snow, whatever—she walked to town to work and back
again. After my parents, and I, left Eastland and Maifred got a
job in the Court of Civil Appeals, she moved into a room in the
Connellee Hotel. I figured she did that because she was sick of
walking to work. The hotel was just a block from her desk in the
courthouse.

Leo Wolf used to hang around our kitchen where Mama would
introduce him to pork products he didn't get at home, where his

Jewish grandmother did the cooking and everything she fixed was kosher.

Mama seemed to get satisfaction out of feeding Leo bacon and eggs or a ham sandwich. I used to wonder why, but she wouldn't talk about it much. To me it seemed out of character that she failed to respect the rules and regulations of a religion other than hers.

No friends I made in Eastland were as dear to me as the Galloways. The Entire Family. Mr. and Mrs. Rip Galloway and their several children. Their son Jim was a year ahead of me in school, and his brother Bob was a year behind me, and I always felt I fit into that bunch, in there between Jim and Bob. The family was just wonderful to me. It's almost embarrassing, thinking about it now.

When I was in college in Lubbock my parents had left Eastland. On holidays I would hitchhike back to the old county seat and go to the Galloways on Seaman Street, just as if I belonged there. They never treated me like a guest. When I showed up it was like they were saying, "Hey, where you been so long? Come on in."

I always felt super-close to two other Eastland families. One was the Wiegands—Herman and Adele and their two daughters, Patsy and Betty. The other family was Cousin Dixie Williamson and her daughter Alma.

My family was supposed to be kin to Dixie, via marriage way back down the line, and that's why we called her cousin.

I spent a good deal of time at both those houses but not for the same reason I hung out with the Galloways. The girls, they were the real reason. At one time or another I was in love, or thought I was, with both Patsy and Betty and Alma as well. But they were all pretty girls and good dancers so there was a lot of competition, from guys who had access to cars. I was forever afoot, or on a bicycle, and looking for somebody with wheels who'd let me double date.

Patsy Wiegand was the second girl I kissed. (The first was Jimmie May Mitchell. Forty years later at a reunion I saw Jimmie and asked if she remembered me kissing her and she didn't, which hurt my feelings because that smooch was a big event in my life.)

While I was overseas, fighting to save the American way of life, I was still writing love letters to Patsy. Then she wrote back and told me to stop because she was married. So I switched to her sister Betty and started writing to her, and the same thing soon happened. Before I bought any more stamps I did check to see if Cousin Alma was still available. I learned that she was already married to a doctor in Houston. So that wiped out all my Eastland girlfriends. Well, I was in love with Tizzy Sikes for quite a while, and Gerry Russell for a month or two but she disappeared into the student body of a fancy university Up East and has never been seen again, at least not by me.

I need to stop and do my chores.

29 MARCH

In the last two days, the live oaks here in the yard at Winedale have broken out in those pale green frangey-pangey globes they use for blooms. This is good news, especially since the two big trees we thought were dying are doing their best to bloom with all the others. If we can save those old sweethearts, that's all the success I'd have the guts to ask for this year. We do love those trees.

Babette is working on her novel, line by line, word by word. She has a fine story and I think it'll be published if we can get it into the hands of the right agent/editor/publisher. The book is close to finished. Right now she's just going back through, tweaking, trying to make it perfect. Babette is a pro writer with a remarkable command of the language, and I've never known anyone who works harder. I mean every day, often at night. If she finds fifteen minutes, she goes to the computer and works on her book or her short stories. She deserves success.

This morning I am concerned about the health of both of us. She has developed a stomach problem and must be super-careful about what she eats.

Me, I don't know what to think about how I'm doing. I just got the detailed results from my recent annual physical and for a dude of my age, my numbers are good and some are excellent. But I don't feel so hot. The A-fib keeps me weak-kneed, and I have that aortic aneurysm that seems stable but it can't be making me feel any better.

Doctor says I'm very active for ninety-three (hey, ninety-four in May) and it's true I can move around, but you have to give me time to prepare. I've been sitting here now for two hours, and if a grizzly bear came in and offered to eat me I could not leap up and run away. He would need to give me thirty seconds to rise, and stand, and get some circulation going in my legs. Then if he were a fair bear he'd let me have about a hundred yard head start before he charged.

30 MARCH

Hello from the bathroom. I'm spending a lot of time in here lately. Reason is, my recent physical showed that I need to drink more water. So every time I think about it, I drink water. I pour it in, and out it comes.

At night, too. I meet myself in the hall, either coming or going, every two hours. What great fun. Old age is nothing but a bitter laugher.

Here's the first journal entry written in my new Winedale front-porch office. I may end up really loving this place. I feel like I'm outside, so close to the flowers and shrubs and trees, and yet I'm behind clear glass, with AC that'll be a sweet luxury this summer.

Today I'm watching an avian conflict. We have a bluebird nesting box on the front yard fence. It was used last year, and just a minute ago a pretty blue (maybe a parent from last year) flew in and stuck its head in the hole and guess what—the box is already occupied, by a pair of chickadees.

Now if this bluebird were a purple martin it would chase those chickadees off and clear out their nest. But bluebirds are nice gentle creatures and I doubt they'll do anything to these interlopers. Probably means we won't have bluebirds this year. Too bad, because we've already got plenty of chickadees, and they're becoming so bold they sit on fence posts early in the morning and fuss at me for being so slow about putting out sunflower seed.

Becky e-mailed yesterday and asked me to write an excuse to her bridge teacher for her absence from a lesson. So I wrote it. "Dear Mr. ---------: Please excuse Becky's absence from her bridge lesson today. She is not feeling well." I gather that's some kind of joke. First excuse of that kind I've written since the kids were in grade school.

For the last week we've been back in Houston entertaining a visiting two-and-a-half-year-old visitor from New York City, Declan Warren, Babette's grandson. He brought with him his parents, Maren and Will Warren, who labor mightily in the Manhattan vineyards.

They have ordered up a little sister for Declan, due for delivery next August, I believe. This event, I bet, will become a thundering blow to Declan's existence.

He is a super-smart little actor who enjoys performing for any adoring audience. At the age of two he is reciting the alphabet without a bobble and singing Old MacDonald Had a Farm, populated by creatures he has seen at the zoo, like lions and tigers and three-toed sloths. He can already work puzzles the complexity of which confound me. And when that little sister comes squalling onto the stage, demanding attention—hoo-boy, Declan will look upon her in shock and awe. What's this? Another baby? In this same world?

He calls me Papa Hale. This moniker was put into his vocabulary by his Houston grandmother, who answers to Grah'MERE, which is the way I pronounce grandmother in French. The French like to scatter apostrophes and other curious marks here and there in their words that way. Nobody knows why.

It's a good thing this kid is smart or he'd never stay straight on how to address all his kinfolks. In addition to Grah-MERE he has Opa, who is the father of Declan's father who was once married to Grah-MERE. So Opa is his paternal grandfather who is now married to Oma who becomes Declan's step-grandmother.

Then in the state of New York he has Pop-pop who is the father of his mother and therefore his maternal grandfather whose wife is Nana who rides horses. Then I came along and met Grah-MERE who was without a husband at the time and kept wanting one, so I volunteered to take that position and this converted me into Declan's step-grandfather and got me that Papa Hale name.

I don't object to being called Papa. Both my own kids call me Papa, or anyway they did when they were young. But I know how Babette's head works on such matters. When she was deciding what her grandchild should call her husband, she threw out Papa because to most people that name implies fatherhood. So she added Hale in honor of my own family and I became Papa Hale to Declan and that's all right.

Not everybody in my family is fond of the name Papa. When he got into high school, Mark quit Papa and began calling me Pop and he still does. I know how his mind works, too. He felt Papa was too childish, or maybe way too old-fashioned, and he couldn't stand for his peers to hear him using it, so he cut it short.

I went through a similar experience with my own father. To Maifred and Ima Ruthie he was Daddy and I called him Daddy as well but eventually I just couldn't stand that term. It seemed like a sugary old Southernism to me so I changed him to Pop, just as Mark did. We never discussed the change but the letters my father wrote me when I was overseas were signed Pop, not Daddy.

Enough about Papa/Daddy names. How did I get started on that?

Today I can sense/hear notes of celebration from two sources. The celebration I can hear comes from Babette who is laughing and clapping and cheering because Tony Doerr's fine novel, 'All the Light We Cannot See,' has just won the Pulitzer Prize for Literature.

Babette is a huge Doerr fan. Calls him a writer's writer. I agree, damn right. That 'All the Light' book is a wonderful story.

The other celebration I can only sense, because it's going on a hundred miles away, in the Chronicle Building in Houston. One of our staff columnists, Lisa Falkenburg, has won the Pulitzer for Commentary. First Pulitzer for the *Chronicle*.

Eight years ago when Lisa, then 28, came to the *Chronicle* we all knew this girl was somebody special. In her column her target was injustice, here in a state that's overflowing with wrongdoing, and she pursued it with liberal red-haired passion. Way to go, Lisa. We're all so proud of you.

This morning I went into Round Top for groceries and mail and, for the first time, I needed a cane to walk safely. I didn't have one, and came close to falling in the parking lot of the Post Office.

Ever since I turned seventy I've had canes, three or four of them, leaning in a corner. I've thought, a time or two, that I better take one along when I'd start into unfamiliar territory. Took one to New York City one time, and it was just in the way. I was always dropping the thing, causing pedestrians to walk around me, or stop and pick it up for me. Once on the airplane I let the cane poke out in the aisle and a fat guy came along and tripped on it. Didn't fall, but he almost did. A cane needs management.

This past week in Houston I turned up with something seriously the matter with my left knee, so that I could hardly walk on it. This is the joint that's given me trouble before, by threatening to collapse when I put my full weight on it. It has, in fact, fully collapsed one time, when I was carrying groceries into this old house, and I went sprawling onto the stone walk. That was more than a year ago and I've still got sore places from that fall. The wonder is that I didn't break my fool neck.

After this morning's experience, I'm putting a cane in my pickup and I intend never again to be without one. If I become an ancient old dude—all bent over, creeping along with a walking stick—so be it.

Tonight Babette made something I like. Ground buffalo meat mixed in a big iron skillet with canned tomatoes and poured over capellini pasta and sprinkled with grated parmesan. She makes this sometimes with rice instead of pasta but it always has a deep nutty flavor. I think the secret is the spices she adds. I lose track of what they are. I suspect you can't just USE spices. You've got to know which to put in what, and when, and how much of each.

5 MAY

I remember the first time I ever crossed the Rio Grande. From McAllen I went across to Reynosa and had a tequila sour for one peso, which was fifteen cents at the time, and I ate my first *cabrito*, too.

A great celebration was going on, and I asked a clerk in a gift shop what the big party was about and she said, "Oh, señor, it is the Five of May."

So this is Mexican Independence Day, May 5, the same for them as Fourth of July is for us.

Our latest problem: Babette is suffering from a case of shingles, which as everyone should know can be a plenty serious and highly painful disease. I don't mind admitting this scared me, when I saw that awful shingles rash crawling across Babette's face, just under her eye. Shingles rash tends to become crusty and nasty and can result in permanent scars. Scars? On that beautiful skin? We can't have that.

We headed for Houston and spent a week going to doctors. And right now I can say maybe she's been lucky. Apparently she got the anti-viral med in time to stop the spread of the rash, and she's looking lots better, and docs say there'll be no scars. But shingles symptoms have a nasty habit of hanging around, causing discomfort sometimes for months, even years.

In 1939, my freshman year in college, I had what was diagnosed as shingles—a painful rash on the back of my neck. I was treated with vitamin injections. Don't recall which vitamin. Back of my neck still has little bump-scars from that case.

Worst thing about it was that somebody scared the whey out of me with this old wives tale: If you get the shingles rash on your waist, and it goes all around your body and meets on the other side to form a shingles circle, you die immediately.

As a college freshman I was believing everything I heard, and all that year when I showered I inspected my torso for signs of rash.

13 MAY

Weather, weather, weather. We've having it, in spades and hearts. A monster low pressure cell has stalled over lower West Texas and is sending us pockets of rain all through the state, from southwest to northeast. been going on for three days and it's not finished yet. Neighbors are saying that the drouth is over. I hope they're still saying that in August.

We're under a tornado watch right now, but the heavy rains have missed us so far. I doubt we've had two inches. Becky and Mark, down in Houston's Clear Lake area, had four inches just last night.

I'm reading Helen Macdonald's *'H is for Hawk'* book, about falconry, and grief, and I'm not sure what else. Like most Brit writers Macdonald can handle the language beautifully, but in this book she is telling me more about falconry than I need to know. Or at least she's mighty slow about getting around to telling me what I do want to know about it.

I like hawks. We have plenty of them around Winedale. A pair of Cooper's hawks—I am guessing at that identification—is raising a family in our patch of woods. Or maybe across the fence in Henry Ullrich's pasture. I haven't located the nest but almost every morning I hear the hawks fussing when they circle over the treetops.

The wind has stirred the live oaks in the yard and the rain has started a heavy drumming on the metal roof. So I leave the journal quickly and jump on the Internet to see if anything dangerous might be headed our way. If the genie rose out of the bottle and offered me one wish, I would wish my father here beside me for just a minute, so I could show him this:

Out here in these woods, a hundred miles from Houston, if I need to know what's going on with the weather I simply turn on this computer. It will tell me if rain is in the area, and whether it is likely to fall on our place, and whether the rain will be heavy or medium or light. The computer will alert me if the weather is about to turn violent. If a tornado is spinning in the area, this machine is capable of showing it to me. Where it is. Even which direction it's traveling, so that we can take cover if it's coming our way. True, for these tech wonders to happen everything has to be working right and sometimes everything doesn't. But I'd love to study my father's face when he watches the screen while I show him how I check the weather.

This was a man who thought the water heater was among the greatest of all inventions. To him, even a radio was a marvel. He never ceased to wonder that he could turn on the little receiver beside his bed in West Texas and hear Bob Burns playing the bazooka in Nashville, Tenn.

Nothing remarkable is happening with the weather right now, so back to whatever we were talking about.

Hawks? Well, enough about hawks.

Have I written about our new Post Office box? Couple of weeks ago I went into Round Top and asked the postmaster, Laura Davis, if she had a mail box for rent, one with a good number. Told her I was superstitious about numbers. She said, "How about Box 77? It became available just yesterday." Told her I'd take it.

I'm so pleased to get that box, because seventy-seven is a cool number. Such a box should draw good mail with lots of positive information. Checks, maybe, with many zeros.

For the last thirty-odd years I've had P.O. Box 130828 in Houston and I've never liked the number. There's nothing distinctive about it. Nobody can remember it, and I'm gradually retiring it. We spend more and more time up here at Winedale, and we've been paying our helper Maureen to pick up mail and send it up here, and that gets expensive.

Round Top is five miles from here but one of us goes there just about every day, so picking up mail is no big problem. I've always liked going to the Post Office anyway. Because that's where you see people that need seeing, and hear things that need hearing.

Oh, we'll still get some mail to our RFD box out of Burton, delivered to us six days a week by the carrier. We do like the carrier. She's a friendly blonde lady who sometimes, when it's raining, will turn in the front gate and bring mail to the house. Drives a Jeep.

When I write or even mention rural mail carriers I travel all the way back to Grandma Hale's place and the bizarre time we spent there during the Depression.

All of us, adults and kids both, often spoke the name Claude Boles, who carried the mail out of the Gordon Post Office.

To us he was a high-ranking government official, the highest, anyway, that we knew personally. I remember being sent to the mail box to wait for him and buy a two-cent stamp. When he gave me three pennies change out of a nickel, our fingers brushed, and I told about that at the house, about touching the hand of Mr. Boles.

On most days, his old sedan was the only motorized vehicle that passed in front of Grandma's house. We watched for him, listened for the sound of his engine.

On rainy days the boys would say, "Well, ol' Claude'll have to put his mud chains on this mornin'."

Mr. Boles would be mentioned on the porch after supper, when the men spoke of hard times. You'd hear, "Claude Boles don't even know a Depression's goin' on. The first day of ever' month, Uncle Sam sends him a check for ninety dollars."

I wonder now if that amount was anywhere near right. Maybe so. I can recall men talking about working for a dollar a day, and glad to be getting it. When Maifred landed a position at the weekly Eastland Record—while the other members of our family were hiding from the world at Grandma's farm—her salary was five dollars a week, and sometimes she got it two or three weeks late.

8 JUNE

Look at that date. I haven't made an entry in this journal for more than a week. The reason is, Babette put me back to work for a while.

Winedale Publishing has decided to re-issue a book of mine that's been out of print for several years. It's the little *One Man's Christmas* book, which sold pretty well. When the holidays come around we always hear from people who have the book and who put it out on their coffee table at Christmas.

This is a hint that for a few folks, at least, *One Man's Christmas* has become a cult book. So with this new issue we'll give it a chance to become a cult book for a lot of people.

Babette (remember she's editor of Winedale Publishing) decided to change the content of the book and I had to write a new piece to go in it, and man, did I have a hard time. Grinding out a 1,500-word story helped me see clearly how I have lost steps as a writer. I'm not able to see my mistakes the way I once could. I fill my stuff with little old conversational cliches that I fail to catch, and I've lost lots of words that I still need, and my spelling has become truly creative.

These are common shortcomings for a person my age so I'm not much concerned about them. Before I quit the column and retired, I knew this was happening, but I didn't know how bad it was. Babette could surely see it, and Luman, my copy editor. Oh well, so I'm slipping at ninety-four. Everybody has to slip eventually.

14 JUNE

Just now noticed, by accident, that I began this journal one year ago today.

We've just about wrapped up preparation for the re-issue of the little Christmas book, or at least we've done everything that I need to be involved in. I am properly sick at my belly at its content, after we combed through it line by line and fixed whatever needed fixing. There's a popular belief that writers are in love with their own prose. But in the case of books, if they aren't sick of them before they ever come out, they haven't spent enough time polishing and tweaking.

The last few years we've hired a contractor to come and mow the Winedale place, and do the edging in the yard, and prune Babette's roses and bushes. I used to do all that myself but now it's way too much for me. I've got a good eight-horse riding mower and I can get it going and mow inside the yard, which is one acre. I've got a big weed eater, too, for edging, but it's too heavy for me now.

So Nick the contractor comes regularly with his Hispanic labor and they ride these huge mowers that cut a swath about five feet wide and make a racket like a flock of bulldozers. For four hours they're here, and our experience is that the noise they make and the vibration they create in the air stirs up snakes in the yard and beneath the house.

We do have snakes. They den up in armadillo holes and lie around in the bushes. And under the house. A fellow at the hardware store in Round Top wanted to sell me some snake repellent. "Put this stuff under your house you'll git rid of them snakes."

But wait a minute, Elroy, the snakes are under the house, minding their own business. I hit 'em with that repellent, they'll come out. I don't want 'em out. I want 'em to stay under there and be happy.

Most of these reptiles are rat snakes, which help us control rodents and we don't bother them. Some are copperheads, and sometimes we have to kill one of those when they get in our way.

If a snake ever harms me here at Winedale, it won't be because it bites me. It'll be because it startles me, and I'll try to move rapidly out of its way. I don't move rapidly anymore, and my big feet will get in each other's way, and I'll fall, and break something important, or cause something important to stop working, and that'll be the end of me.

Moving along, we're coming up on Round Top's famous Fourth of July Celebration. This is the Big One for the Round Top area. Bigger even than Christmas. Maybe even bigger than Mother's Day Weekend, which is super-huge.

Everybody has their yard mowed and trimmed and their flags flying and their pickups washed and polished and their baths taken and their whiskers shaved and their hair frizzed up. There'll be a great parade and barbecues and beer-drinking and dances and speeches and stirring marches from the local brass band led by Ronnie Sacks, president of the Round Top State Bank. At the height of the celebration you can feel the patriotism pouring out of all those broad chests and bulging stomachs. How fortunate they feel, to live in this great country which has no equal in the universe, or Heaven, either, a nation which may have one or two faults but not today, at least not in Round Top, Texas.

Back before this celebration became so large, I was invited to make a Fourth of July speech, there on the Round Top town square. Did I accept? Yes, indeed, and my address was well received by the throng, which rewarded me with prolonged applause peppered with shouts and whistles. And the reason was, I talked for only two minutes.

Today no newspaper columnist would ever be asked to speak at this celebration. Congressmen come, instead. Senators. Billionaires. Pro football players. And the rumor is that this year Governor Goodhair Himself will appear, and address the multitude. This may, in fact, come to pass because His Majesty has bought land near Round Top, and built a pleasure palace there, and he's running for president.

Think of this, folks. We're facing the possibility that the most passionate fantasy of Round Top people could become reality. That great house He built at Blossom Hill, not three miles from the center of town, could one day soon be the President's summer home, and He would come to us, and dwell among us.

Is this not possible? Not a fortnight past didn't his very wife appear at the Rifle Hall where Round Toppers gather on Monday nights? And didn't she have a hamburger heavy on the mustard and wasn't she heard to say, "A hamburger without onion is not a hamburger"? Is this not so?

What disturbs my sleep, a little, is that we are at least approaching the possibility that Rick Perry could become president of the United States. He is, more than anything else, an effective politician.

I'm trying to think of something worse than Perry in the White House. Donald Trump in there, maybe? Russia dropping a hydrogen bomb on the Houston Ship Channel? There, that would be worse. I guess.

12 JULY

Things have been pretty quiet here in the woods, since the big Fourth of July Celebration. Governor Goodhair disappointed the Round Toppers by not showing up for the parade, as he had threatened.

My old Timex is reading seven P.M. on this fair day, which is Babette's seventy-first birthday. We have now been together, as the saying is, for thirty-four years.

She received gifts, and a pleasant ride over the green countryside with her favorite husband, who bought her a slice of Forbidden Pecan Pie in Orzak's Cafe in Fayetteville. Then a birthday supper of tuna fish salad prepared by her FH and served with a chilled bottle of non-alcoholic beer. How fortunate she is.

14 JULY

In our living room/library here at the Winedale place we have 750 books, the usual items of furniture, and a new Schwinn stationary bicycle (recumbent). The bike is not yet broken in but I think from my limited experience with it that it's making my arthritic knees better, and my weak/stiff legs, too.

This is important right now because in about a week Babette and I will get on an airplane and fly to Sewanee, Tenn. where she will attend a two-week writers conference.

And so we now come to the Big Question, faced by couples with large age differences such as Babette's and mine. I'm ninety-four. She's a young seventy-one. The question is, What To Do With the Old Man?

I'm not entirely out of the game, yet. But I have this heart condition, and a few other health issues, and I'm getting close to the point that I can't travel very far. Except for short distances, walking is a problem, and if you can't walk, you're better off staying home.

Babette has health problems of her own but they're not as limiting as mine, and she's not ready to stay home.

Her abiding interest is her writing. She can afford the expense of this conference, and there's no reason she shouldn't go. So what's the problem?

The problem is that she won't go without me.

Before I turned ninety, she would go off on trips that had to do with her family business, or one of her writing projects, and leave me alone for two, maybe three nights. I got along all right by myself, but that was before.

Now, she's hesitant about leaving me alone even for one night. So if she wants to travel, I either agree to go with her, or she stays home. I hate it, when I've become a burden this way.

Could I get along all right, alone, for two weeks? I think probably I could, but at the apartment in Houston, not up here at Winedale. The terrain here is a trifle rough, making a serious fall way too likely. If I fell, say, out in the yard and couldn't get up, that would probably be the end of me because cell phones work here maybe half the time. That's a moot point anyway because Babette's not gonna leave me alone in the country.

Now two weeks alone in the Houston apartment might work OK. Falling with a cell phone on the sixth floor? Cell phone works fine at that elevation, and we have 24-hour staff people who could load me into an ambulance if I needed hospitalizing.

Then we have Mark and Becky, who would come and stay with me here in the country or in Houston.

When her first grandbaby was born, Babette went to New York for a week and I stayed at Becky's and Mark took me fishing and we cooked good stuff that I'm not supposed to eat and I drank more than I'm supposed to drink and it was all great fun.

But I could tell even that one week got long for both of them. I've never planned on my children taking care of me in my old age. I've told Babette, stick me in the nearest nursing home but don't dump me onto Mark and Becky. Oh, they love me and they'd take me but I don't want to complicate their lives by asking them to play nurse-maid to an old man.

What I started out to say is that when Babette goes to that shindig in Tennessee, I'm gonna get on the airplane and go with her.

14 AUGUST

Check the date above. Exactly a month has rolled by since my last journal entry.

Yes, we made the flying trip to Tennessee and back, and saw some beautiful Southern forests and had a couple of good adventures and two or three bad ones and we're back now at Winedale and pretty stove up.

I think Babette is happy about going. Her work was read and critiqued by a flock of pro writers, and she met with two New York literary agents and I believe she's encouraged. I am anyway.

What I did mainly in Tennessee is get two weeks older. I plowed into some high-salty food and this sent my blood pressure spiking high as smoke, and it's been contrary ever since. This morning it was 123/67 and any doctor and his nurse would tell you that's about as close to a normal reading as I'll ever manage. But if I took another reading right now, at eleven-thirty A.M., it might be 148/82, or even much higher. And sometimes it nose-dives. Within the last week I've measured it at 90/57, and I had to quit taking my BP pills, and take on a little salt, and black coffee. Management of my BP has become a sort of avocation.

5 SEPTEMBER

Last few weeks we've been sweating out results of medical tests, that we underwent soon after returning from Tennessee. I turned up so close to total dehydration that the nurse had trouble drawing enough blood out of me to do any testing. So now I'm force-feeding water. I'm supposed to get at least six six-ounce glasses of the stuff down me every day, and I promise you that's a chore.

Good news, though, on other fronts. Friends of Winedale, (Babette Hale, President,) flung its first fund-raising event at Henkel Hall in Round Top and raised something like $230,000, net. This money goes to the University of Texas ear-marked for the improvement of its Winedale Historical Center which is about a mile from where I'm sitting.

Babette's term of office, as president, expires this month and I am glad of that. She'll remain on the board, which is OK. But being president is way too much stress for her (and for me).

We need rain again. Tank is about half empty, mostly from evaporation. Hoping for some cooler temps this month. I'm supposed to have 200 tilapia swimming around in there, but I seldom see any of them.

They may be gradually dying off, during these super-hot days. I once thought that if fish start dying in a tank, I'd know it because they'd float to the surface. But I learned that birds, mostly herons, fly around and check tanks and lakes in hot weather and eat dead fish quick as they come to the surface.

When I had hybrid sunfish in the tank, they all died during a drouth and I never saw one dead fish floating on the surface. Coons, as well as birds, will help clean up dead fish.

No sign of cooler weather yet. High for today, ninety-five.

Watched a good ball game yesterday. Astros belted a couple of homers in late innings and beat the Twins 8-5. They're still leading the West Division by three games.

Today they're en route to Anaheim, on a ten-day road trip. I figure if they can get back home after this trip and still have even a one-game lead in the division, we'll see 'em in the play-offs, with a chance at the World Series. But they've had a hard time winning on the road, and they need to find a way to beat the Rangers. They have four games with the Rangers, in Arlington, on this trip.

Tonight Babette's going to one of her story-reading meetings so I'll open a can of pinto beans and doctor 'em up with chili powder and chopped onion and a few drops of Balsamic vinegar and maybe an ounce or two of molasses. Pour in a good deal of low-salt chicken broth. (I like lots of juice.) A little thyme. A little cumin. Maybe a little garlic powder.

Babette won't eat pintos but I need 'em at least once a month to remind me where I came from.

Astros are dying. Lost two in a row on the current road trip and their division lead is down to one game. They're a power-hitting team. Power teams hit a lot of home runs but they fan a lot, too. I wouldn't bet much money on 'em when they're facing really good pitching. Which they would see in most play-off games.

We keep running into interesting people up here in Washington and Fayette counties. Emmy, for example, and Elvis. They've both worked for us, Emmy as an excellent maid and Elvis as a not so excellent gardener. Don't ask me their last names.

They are Belizeans. From the Central American nation of Belize, that is. We have a lot of these people in the area. Who knows how many?

When you and I studied geography, Belize was on the map as British Honduras, a colony of England. Belize is an independent nation now but in school its children still get English as a first language.

With their English these migrant Belizeans come in here and do well. They are intelligent, handsome people. I'm told that some local contractors, such as stone masons and landscape gardeners, don't like the Belizeans because they'll work for the contractors about a year, learn the business, then quit and start businesses of their own, as tough competitors.

Emmy was probably the best maid we ever had. She was with us several years but has gone back home now and we do miss her.

Elvis is still here, and has a steady job at Festival Hill in Round Top. He says his father named all the sons in the family after famous entertainers.

I was behind Elvis in line at the Round Top Post Office yesterday. He was carrying on a lively conversation with Postmaster Laura Davis, in Spanish. Most of the Belizeans speak Spanish as well as English and a few, I hear, get along in various other tongues, or dialects.

Laura Davis speaking Spanish surprised me. I asked her where she got it and she said, "Argentina. I was born in Argentina."

Now that's really interesting because she also speaks English with a German brogue, much like we hear from the locals of Round Top, many of whom are descended from German immigrants. This suggests that our postmaster was raised in Argentina by German-speaking parents.

11 SEPTEMBER

Fourteen years ago at this hour, two events were coming to pass, and I wish neither of them had ever happened.

One was the destruction of the Twin Towers, which changed this entire country forever. The other was, we were moving out of Babette's house on Stanmore, to live in the high-rise apartment on San Felipe.

We should never have left that house. It needed a lot of money spent on it but we could have borrowed what we needed and made the improvements. By now, we'd have paid off the debt and Babette would have the home she still wants.

I blame myself for that bad move. I was simply not comfortable living in River Oaks, among all those wealthy people. What a stupidity that was.

Nobody cares where I live. And anyway, that house on Stanmore was modest. I bet it was the only two-bedroom home in River Oaks, and yet when I was asked where I lived I'd catch myself saying "near the intersection of Kirby Drive and San Felipe." To keep from saying "River Oaks." How dumb was that?

21 SEPTEMBER

We've both undergone just about all the medical testing we can stand. It's tempting to conclude that doctors are putting us through tests that we don't need. However, in my case, history says I'm alive right now because of testing. Tests discovered the cancerous tumor on my colon, and tests discovered the cancerous tumor in my bladder. And surgery took care of both those, and either of them could have killed me by now. So I guess if the docs say test, I'll test.

Another nice salad for supper. Lately we've been buying "living lettuce," which comes in a plastic container. The head has been pulled up by the roots, which are enclosed in the package so the plant is still alive and growing and even the outside leaves are tender and crisp. Sure, it's expensive but we eat it all, right down to the roots. Don't throw those outside leaves away, like we do on regular lettuce.

29 SEPTEMBER

Once again drama invades the lives of the Hale family.

Babette was ticketed and already packing to fly up to NY and see Maddie, her latest grandchild. (Madeleine, that is.) And Becky was loaded up to come to Winedale and stay with me for a few days while Babette was gone.

So naturally the dog got sick.

Came down with kennel cough. The most awful gasping cough. KC is not an especially dangerous disease but it's tricky to treat. There are viral forms of it and there are bacterial forms and some of these are easily transmissible to humans, especially babies and very elderly adults. And the bugs are hard to get rid of. That is, they cling to your clothes, and if you've lately had any close association with a KC-infected dog, you shouldn't go near a small child. This is what we were told.

Have we had any recent close association with this Rosie dog? Well, how about sleeping with her on the same bed, Doctor? And Babette about to fly to NY to see her grandchild who is eight weeks old?

So the trip was called off, and Becky won't be coming to Winedale, least not for a while.

Better news: Rosie quit coughing almost immediately after she took her first dose of medicine.

Even better news: One of Babette's short stories, titled "Drouth," has been recognized as a "distinguished American short story" in the anthology "Best American Short Stories." (Her story was published by *Southwest Review*.) This is significant national recognition, and we celebrated on the back porch. I drank my daily five-ounce glass of wine, and Babette downed a cold bottle of Texas Special, which is a non-alcoholic beer.

Then more news, which I'll call only *pretty* good: *One Man's Christmas*, our little paperback holiday book coming forth from Winedale Publishing, is showing "Sold Out" by Amazon, the huge internet retailer. That's pretty good instead of really good because we don't know how many books Amazon had to begin with. (Probably about twenty-five copies, be my guess.) We'll know more within a month when the promotional material, just now going out, does its work, if any.

Still more news, which I'll risk calling *good*: We're beginning to get some October weather here in October. Beautiful cool mornings, and maybe no more of those condemned ninety-degree afternoons.

More news yet, and *good* for certain: HEB in Brenham has brought in a shipment of big honey-crisp apples, and they are double-dee-licious.

Good news, continued: I cooked a great pot of pinto beans, with onion and chili pepper and Washington County well water. And two slices of ham, cut up, because I couldn't locate a chunk of salt pork. And toward the end this woman came in and took the lid off the pot and sniffed and put in cumin, lots of it, and oregano, and two cloves of garlic, and thyme, and a little more salt.

These are such lovely beans. I'm going to Round Top and buy

some little plastic containers and save these beans in the freezer. I may be eating on them until Thanksgiving. Babette is hell on putting flavor into pintos but she doesn't eat very many. That's because the French haven't yet discovered that they are edible.

5 OCTOBER

Good news just keeps on a-comin'. The Astros have clinched a wild card spot in the American League championship play-offs. They'll face the New York Yankees up there in the Bronx tomorrow night. This is a one-game play-off, with the winner staying alive in competition for the American League Pennant and a shot at the World Series.

The thing is, just three years ago it was not even reasonable to talk about the Astros playing the New York Yankees for any reason whatever, except maybe in spring training. Then suddenly the suits that control professional baseball decided that Houston's team ought to play in the American League instead of the National.

Astro fans cried foul. Come on, we can't play in that league, with the Yankees and the Red Sox and that snooty bunch. They don't even play the same kind of baseball. We'll be five years learning how to win games in the American League. We've been screwed.

And sure enough, our guys stayed mostly in the cellar of the West division for a couple of seasons.

Then they started picking up some young talent in the draft, and finally hired the right field manager, and suddenly, look who's sitting at the top of the west division for most of the 2015 season— the Astros.

True, they faded seriously in September but revived toward the end of the season, won some tough games on the road, and here they are en route to NY to play the Yankees.

They already know they can beat the Yanks. They did it early in the season, twice, and in Yankee Stadium, at that. They haven't yet figured out how to beat the Rangers but we can't get everything done in one year.

I'm hungry.

6 OCTOBER

More good news. Astros beat the Yankees, 3-0. Now they move on to Kansas City to challenge the Royals, who played in the World Series last year.

7 OCTOBER

Even more good news. Astros beat the Royals, 5-2. If they can do that one more time, they'll come back home needing only one more win in this three out of five series against KC and we'll have our ace on the mound. This is getting really interesting.

10 OCTOBER

Damn. Bad news. Astros lost to KC.

However, the Royals have still got to face Kuechel in Sunday's home game.

Now here's what you might call a nice little good-news story:

About 40 years ago, my friend Merck Smith of Louise, TX bought a piece of vacant prairie down on the coast, near Port Lavaca. He divided it up into one-acre lots, a subdivision, and called it Bluebonnet Acres.

When he was selling those lots, for around $1,000 a copy, I was down that way and I stopped by and had a beer with Merck, asked him how his lots were selling. Little slow, he said.

Then he said, "How'd you like to own one of my lots? I'll give you one."

I thought he was kidding and didn't even answer.

"No, come on, I'm serious," he said. "I'll give you this corner lot, which fronts on the blacktop. It'll sit there and increase in value. It's a good lot."

I asked him why he'd do such a thing and he said, "It'll help me sell the other lots. I'll put a sign in the middle of it, with your name on it."

I told him no, I couldn't do that. People would think I've gone in the real estate business.

He said, "No they wouldn't. It wouldn't be a for-sale sign. It'd just show your name, two words, and nothing else. People would think it's a lot that Leon Hale bought, in Bluebonnet Acres. You'd be doing me a favor. What's wrong with that? "

Well, I thought about it a while, and I didn't see anything wrong with it, at that. So Merck gave me the lot, and put up the sign with my name on it, and I became a landowner in Calhoun County. I've been paying taxes on the lot since the 1970s, about $100 a year.

I never did see the sign, except in a picture that Merck took and sent to me. I doubt it helped sell any lots because about a week after it went up, somebody stole it.

To help you understand why Merck would give away a piece of his property that way, you need to know about one of the many curiosities that exist in the column-writing game:

After a columnist has been working long enough to enjoy a considerable following, he/she will acquire a handful of what you might call super fans. Maybe just four or five people, who love every line the columnist writes, and who think that everybody else in creation should feel the same way.

Merck was the foremost of my little bunch of super fans. You don't want many, because they can become truly high maintenance. But they can be valuable, since they'll do almost anything to help you do a day's work.

I had mixed feelings about going to see Merck. I liked going because he was good company, and always pleased when I showed up. But being with him could be embarrassing.

Because he would want to go around with me and introduce me to friends. And when we met one who had never heard of me, much less read my column or my books, he wasn't above scolding them, for not being my fan. (I doubt this gained me any readers.)

Merck loved my beer-joint novel, *Bonney's Place*, and simply wouldn't accept that it was not "made into a movie." He stayed angry about this. It was almost as if that unmade film represented a major failure on his part.

So maybe you understand, now, why he'd give me that piece of property. Hey, this is the guy who built a room onto his house, for me, so I'd have a place to stay when I was working in his area. He called it the Leon Hale bedroom, in which I never spent a night.

When Merck was dying with cancer, he asked me to write a few lines about him, to be read by the preacher at his funeral. I wish now I'd saved that short paragraph. I remember I had a hard time getting it done. Merck was a complicated person, difficult to reduce to a few short sentences.

Gradually Merck and his friendship became a fading memory, which annually came rising out of the past when I received the tax notice on my lot from the Calhoun County assessor. The $100 a year wasn't a huge problem but 100 bucks is 100 bucks and every year I'd tell myself I ought to sell that lot.

Occasionally I heard from the people who owned, and lived on, the lot that connected to mine. They wanted to buy my lot but they wanted to get it for practically nothing. The tax appraisal district had a value of $1,500 on the property. My neighbors on the adjacent lot thought that was outrageous and wouldn't pay it.

I decided to give the lot to Merck's widow. But she had died. I got hold of Merck's son and offered to give the lot to him. But he didn't want it. Didn't want anything to do with it.

So I figured I'd donate the thing to the Girl Scouts, or to a country church in the area, or maybe to the favorite charity of Merck Smith, if he had any such interest.

But I never got around to doing what needed to be done. I learned that it's a lot of trouble to give away a piece of property, especially if a tax bill goes along with it. The prospective recipient will say, "Yeah, 100 bucks a year's not high but you know what taxes do, they go up."

For the last several years I almost never gave the lot a stray thought, except when I paid the tax.

Then last spring I got a letter from a woman named Becky Wied, who's in the real estate business down there around Port Lavaca. She wrote that she'd been selling some property along Highway 172 and she wondered if I'd like for her to sell the Merck lot.

I asked how much she thought we could get for it. I figured maybe a couple of grand, maybe three. She said, "Well, an acre lot just down the highway from yours recently sold for $12,000. We could list it for that, see what happens." I told her sure, go ahead, give it a go.

And she sold it, to a woman from San Antonio, for 11,000 bucks.

Well, old Merck Smith, thank you very much. Time I paid the realtor and another minor item among the closing costs, I had more than $10,000 left. Income tax will take a hungry bite out of that but I'll have between $7,000 and $8,000 left, and I've decided to do something unselfish with it, considering it came to me as a gift.

My grandson Travis Hale is a junior at the University of Kansas. I've been helping him with his room and board and books and tuition. Think I'll use the cash from Merck's lot to help push him on through school. Merck would approve of that.

11 OCTOBER

More good news. The Astros whipped Kansas City in Houston today. If they can do it again tomorrow, they'll be playing either Dallas or Toronto for the American League Pennant.

12 OCTOBER

Bad news. They lost today. Now they've got to go back to Kansas City and play the Royals Wednesday in a rubber game. Bummer.

14 OCTOBER

Very bad news. Astros lost, so their season is finished.

15 OCTOBER

Nice cool morning. For first time in months I've felt like going outside to try to do something useful.

Found two flat tires on the riding mower. Pumped them up and they both went flat again. Pumped them up again and shoved short lengths of 4x4 timbers under the frame, so the tires won't rot when they go flat again.

When I feel better than I do today I'll get the lug nuts off those wheels and take 'em into Round Top and have the flats fixed. Do that just any day now.

That little chore made me so tired I rode the golf cart back to the house. I used to go out and work almost all day in the yard, and in the garden, and in the barn, doing stuff that needed doing. No longer. I'm just not able to cut it.

But I do feel energetic enough to climb in the pickup and drive 10 miles over to Carmine and buy a bottle of red vino, of which I can have one glass.

Babette has made me a stack of business-type cards, advertising the coming out of our little Christmas book. I'll go forth, all the way to Round Top (five miles) and hand out these cards to people who look like they might spend sixteen dollars for a book. Makes me feel like I'm running for office, handing out cards that way.

31 OCTOBER

Halloween. We've never had trick or treaters here in the country, so Halloween for us is an ordinary night with no interruptions.

Two years ago we did have some trickers, up on the road. They didn't come to the house. They parked outside our gate, with their lights off, and operated a noise-making device known as a "dumb bull."

This thing is made by stretching a raw animal hide over the end of a 2-foot section of hollow log. A string is attached to the center of the hide, and hangs down through the middle of the hollow. An experienced operator can reach into the hollow, grab the string and run his hand along it, from the top of the hollow to the bottom, and produce a deep beastly roar, audible for half a mile. And plenty scary on a Halloween night. Sounds little like a mad bull, or even an African lion, or some other Something that might eat you alive.

My guess is that this apparatus was built and operated by our neighbor to the north, Randon Dillingham. He probably thought we would be puzzled by the sound, and maybe I would write about it in the column. But it happens I know about dumb bulls, and we ignored the horrible creature that threatened us.

2 NOVEMBER

Blue Bell Ice Cream is coming back to retail shelves, after the company damn near committed suicide by letting disease organisms invade its machinery. While it was shut down I think a multitude of Texans, who'd always thought BB was the only ice cream worth eating, discovered that other brands were as good, and some better.

Babette can't eat ice cream, or at least not much (lactose intolerance), so we don't often have it in the fridge. I would eat the stuff, Blue Bell or any other brand, three meals a day so probably it's good that we're limited.

A big bait of ice cream daily would surely be bad for my blood chemistry and my wounded heart and my waistline. Babette keeps telling me I'm losing muscle weight. And yet when I weigh at the doctor's office I'm still within five pounds of where I've been for twenty years, around 170 naked. Although my doctor weighs me with my clothes on.

There's no doubt that I'm not as strong as I was ten years ago. Doctor Hoermann keeps after me to eat between meals, so I won't fade away like so many super-elderly folks do.

If they'd just let me have a couple of beers every day, instead of this little old one glass of red wine, I'd get stronger. I know I'd be in a better humor.

Here we go into the promotion battle for this little "One Man's Christmas" book. We've survived our first autographing, a pleasant affair with Debbie and Gerald Tobola, at their Copper Shade Tree in Round Top. The weather gave us a kick in the pants with a lot of rain but even so we sold more than a hundred books. I'm here to tell you a hundred books is a good sale, at anybody's autographing.

Now we're headed to Houston.

Since I last wrote in this journal we've had two more autographings, a trip to New York, a virus infection and a family funeral.

On the 14th of November Brazos Bookstore pitched us a big autographing. We had a fine crowd and when the dust settled the next day, the store had sold pretty close to 400 books.

That pleased me a great deal because I wasn't sure anybody in Houston would show up to buy a little LH paperback book selling for sixteen bucks. Brazos is the elite bookstore in Houston. When the heavyweight authors come to town on tour, Brazos is where they come for readings and autographings. Academics from Rice buy expensive books on architecture and art from Brazos.

And it has never stocked my books, which has always irritated me a little. Hey, my wife is part owner of that store, and had a lot to do with saving it a few years ago when it threatened to die.

So it was a nice experience for me to hear Jeremy, Brazos's manager, announce that "One Man's Christmas" was currently the best-selling book in the store. And I notice he has started stocking a few of my old titles, like "Bonney's Place" and "Turn South."

I celebrated that little victory by coming down with some kind of virus, probably picked up from a customer coming through the book-signing line. I wasn't very sick but my timing was bad because this was the week Babette had long-planned a trip to NY to see her new grandgirl.

She offered to cancel on account of my illness but I talked Mark and Becky into coming up to Winedale and baby-sitting me so Babette could go on. I never did get to feeling truly bad so we had a pretty good visit. Lots of football. Lots of talk about the kinfolks, about Helen, about our early times in Bryan and at Camp Creek.

When I got to feeling better we loaded up and drove into Round Top to eat supper at Royer's. Neither of them had ever had that experience, and in this part of the world it's a religiosity that you've never lived if you haven't eaten at Royer's. At least once. Twice is not necessary.

But Royer's for some curious reason was closed so we went to JW's in Carmine where Mark ate a chicken fried steak the size of second base. Said it was good. Maybe it was. My time of eating chicken-fried steaks is past.

Then early on the twenty-ninth my niece Sandi called with the news that Ima Ruthie had died. Just went to sleep and didn't wake up.

She had turned ninety-seven on the 15th of last September. This woman was my closest relative, and the best friend I ever had. When we were growing up, IR and I shared secrets, talked about things we never talked about with anyone else.

In recent times her dementia made communication close to impossible but nobody in my early life was more dear or more significant than Ima Ruthie. Not even Maifred. Not even my parents.

So, I had to go to Eastland, where IR was buried in the family plot. Mama and Fred D. are there. Maifred and Pete are there. Andy and now Ima Ruthie are there.[5] Not me, no. I'll be scattered, and I like the idea of that.

Seems to suit my life.

Not attending that service was unthinkable, for me. It was set for Friday, December 3—square in the middle of our book-signing schedule. We had an autographing set for December 2 in Houston and another for December 4 in Round Top.

Probably I could have driven myself the 250 miles to Eastland for that funeral and saved Babette the torture, but she wasn't about to let me try it, at ninety-four. And it was a trip from hell. Up Highway 36 with delays due to construction, attend the funeral, do the requisite visiting with kinfolks and a sprinkling of old friends, then get back in the car and start home, because we had that book signing set for noon the next day.

We were only twenty minutes late for the autographing, which to me was pretty amazing.

Did I do some of that driving? No, not a mile of it. My driving now makes Babette nervous. Not because I'm such a bad driver but because I'm too slow. Her clock runs faster than mine. At seventy-one her reaction time is still quick and she's a good driver but I doubt I'll ever get accustomed to being a permanent passenger.

Did I consider not going to the funeral? I did think about it, but not for long. It's true that if I had not gone the family would remember me as the brother who didn't attend the funeral of his own sister. But that's not why I had to go. Ima Ruthie is the reason. I feel she'd have known, if I had missed that service.

5. Fred D. Hale was Hale's father; Pete Cullen and Andy Taylor were his brothers-in-law.

I didn't expect to feel much grief or sadness at the funeral and sure enough, I didn't. Nobody else did, either, that I noticed. Maybe they felt the same as I did, that Ima Ruthie had been gone already for the last two years. I didn't even look at the body. Ima Ruthie wasn't in that coffin. I want to remember her at the piano, playing and singing and being happy.

Returning to that church, First Methodist of Eastland, sent me on a trip back into my youth.

Before the service, we attended a nice lunch prepared by the ladies of the church. It was held in what we used to call the basement, a generous space almost as large as the auditorium just above it. I went to Sunday School in there when I was a second grader at West Ward Elementary. They had the space divided up for various classes. My teacher was Dr. Ferguson, a little banty-rooster of a man who always made me uncomfortable by staring at my head.

He had an expression that was central to all his lessons—"fall by the wayside." Every Sunday he told us how we must live Christian lives or else we would fall by the wayside. That was his message. The worst of all things that could come to pass was falling by the wayside.

That meant not getting into heaven. It meant going to hell.

Along about that time I was having trouble with hell. Dr. Ferguson and others had convinced me that even if I *thought* about committing a sinful act, that was the same as actually committing it. This was the rule that would surely send me through the gates of hell in a big red wagon. I had already thought of committing enough sins to sink the Methodist Church into the River Styx. I had even thought of stealing a bicycle from Western Auto.

So, as a graduate of Dr. Ferguson's Sunday School class, I was headed straight down the road to Hades. What saved me was being graduated into Mrs. Crowell's class, which met on the far side of the basement from Dr. Ferguson's. I fell in love with Mrs. Crowell almost immediately because she made the following position statement to her entire class:

She did not believe in hell.

That dear lady would never know what a load she lifted off my spirit. If Mrs. Crowell believed hell didn't exist, I was pleased to match that belief. Come on, Mrs. Crowell wouldn't be sitting in the basement of the First Methodist Church saying such a thing if it weren't so. The Crowells were prominent people in our town. She was president of the Women's Missionary Society, or some such organization of huge importance. Furthermore, her husband ran the lumber yard.

Approximately sixty years after I'd been rescued from hell, in Houston I made a speech to around 600 retirees of Exxon. One of Mr. and Mrs. Crowell's daughters, Frances, was in the audience. In fact, I believe she was the president of that retirees' organization, and had invited me to do that talk.

I was making speeches at this time because I had books to sell and to sell the kind of books I write, you've got to be visible. I made talks to practically every gang of oil company retirees in the south half of Texas, plus the Lions clubs and the Rotarians and the book clubs and the men's breakfast groups and church associations and once a bunch of convicted felons doing time behind the Walls in Huntsville.

Anyhow, in that speech to the Ex-Exxons, I recognized Frances as the daughter of the woman who had saved me from hell, and I thanked her for having Mrs. Crowell for her mama. This was sort of a joke, and yet it was a sincere joke, too. It received thin, scattered laughter.

I could tell right away that a heavy majority of that audience was not comfortable with the idea of a non-existent hell. When you look out at 600 faces and ninety per cent of them instantly change from grins to blanks, you know you've said something unpopular.

Not that this was a serious matter to me. I've told a lot of people my belief on the hell question. I've even written it in the column. When that Ex-Exxon meeting broke up, several preacher-looking gents filed past me with sour expressions and I thought they were going to collar me and talk about my position on hell, but they evidently decided to let it go.

It was good to see Frances again. She was a great dancer in high school. After that meeting we went out and had a couple of beers.

2016

As you see from the dateline just above, this journal has been neglected since early in November. Main reason is that we've been super busy selling the little Christmas book.

Total printing on the book was 3,500 copies and it sold out. Or at least 3,500 copies left the warehouse on their way to book stores. Whether they all left the book stores in the hands of paying customers is another question.

I'm told it'll be probably June before we find out whether we made any money. Why? Because book stores, especially the big ones, are notorious about being slow to pay their bills.

I need to explain our system of selling books, at an autographing. When I say "our" system, I mean Babette's and mine. Here's how it goes, for instance, on one of our good days:

We walk in and maybe a hundred people are standing in line, waiting to buy books. Babette has already had a part in the event, by promoting it. She has posted the place and time on the Internet, sent out press releases and maybe even bought small ads in neighborhood newspapers. She's good at this stuff. Without it there'd be no line, no people. Then for two hours while I sign books she works the line, visiting with the folks who're waiting, looking pretty and telling them how they're gonna like the book.

For supper, chicken enchiladas and guacamole from Los Patrones in Round Top. I rank the 'ladas about a four on a ten scale. For really good Tex Mex we have to go to Houston and

Papasito's on Kirby Drive, and even those 'ladas seldom rank high as eight.

14 MARCH

Comes now a message from my long-time urologist, Bob Light, whom I have not seen in maybe four years. I'm supposed to check in with him annually so I can continue getting the meds that keep my prostate from swelling to the size of a soccer ball. He now reminds me that I'm a little late.

The reason I've avoided him, the last time I was in his office he said I need to get my rupture fixed. (Rupture. At this time I am unable to call up the better term for this condition. It's as simple and familiar to me as the names of my own children but it won't come just now.) This is symptomatic of my growing dementia. At any rate, I call it dementia. Babette disagrees.

The word problem is evident in my speech as well as my thought and my typing. Sometimes I'll have a simple declarative sentence ready to deliver, but it won't arrive. Most times it eventually does, after an embarrassing delay.

The foremost observer of this problem is Babette. When I struggle for words she sometimes gives me drills.

We'll be driving and she'll say, "Look out yonder and tell me what you see."

"Cows in a pasture."

"What kind of cows?"

"Purebred. Those pretty cream-colored cattle."

"The breed. I want the name of the breed."

"I can't think of it. I've written it in the column a thousand times but I can't come up with it now."

"I'll give you a hint. This breed originated in France." (Babette loves anything French. With that hint I am able to bring up the name of the breed.)

"Charolais. I can't believe I couldn't remember that."

"You need to talk more. Who composed Rhapsody In Blue?"

"Gershwin."

"Who Gershwin?"

"George."

"Who was your favorite World War II correspondent?"

"Ernie Pyle."

"Name your favorite World War II cartoon artist."

"Oh. . . don't tell me. Wait. . . He's the fellow who did all those great Willie and Joe cartoons."

"You have a book of them on the shelf right in front of your desk. I saw it yesterday. Part of the title is Up Front."

"Bill Mauldin. I'll never be forgiven for not remembering that name."

Strange pickup coming in front gate. Got to quit.

15 MARCH

Hernia! That's the term I was unable to come up with yesterday. Inguinal hernia. A hernia in the groin area. You'd think I wouldn't have trouble remembering the name of that problem, since I've been walking around with one of the damned things for 10 years, or more.

Sure, it needs to be fixed. We've twice had an appointment to have it done by the best hernia-fixer in the Texas Medical Center, and both times something has happened to cause a cancellation.

One cancellation happened when I had that session of GI bleeding, a little adventure I believe I've already written about in this journal (although I now have trouble remembering what I've written about).

Another cancellation came when Babette had her hip replacement, and getting her past that took more than a year.

Then somewhere along the way I developed this heart problem and at last we got into the question of whether we've waited too late. Am I too far gone to endure surgery? I think the answer is yes.

19 MARCH

Since we talked, I've gone to get my scolding from Dr. Light, the urologist. He has changed. He's unhappy about practicing medicine under the restraints of Medicare and Obamacare. He frowns a lot. He used to laugh, and visit, and tell jokes. He was the doctor who told me about the urologist who stuck two fingers, instead of the customary one, up the behind of a patient. Why? Because the patient wanted a second opinion.

He didn't scold me much. Just changed my medicine and said come back in a year.

27 MARCH

Here at the Winedale place, spring keeps trying to come. We've already had our first ninety-degree day, and the birds are warbling and mating and building nests and the grass is green and the trees are throwing out foliage and we've got a sprinkling of wildflowers on the slope between the house and the front gate.

Then here'll come another cold front to lay a sheet of frost over the landscape and set everything back a few days.

But overall, we haven't had any winter. We had a string of pretty warm days back in February and they were nice and everybody bragged on how wonderful the winter weather was here in Texas.

But spring in February doesn't do us any good. February needs to be cold, and nasty. It's a winter month and ought to quit acting like April.

Journal is two years old today. Happy Birthday, journal.

Took my blood pressure this morning. 148/80. Little high. I'm supposed to keep up with my BP better than I do. It's just something else to worry about, like my teeth and my toenails and my glasses and hearing aids and gall bladder and prostate and all the rest of it.

We gave up our membership in the Forest Club, where Babette had been a tennis-playing member for many years. We quit giving expensive gifts to one another, and we stopped high-flying vacations, such as going to Europe.

Two things had happened almost at the same time, and they pretty well shot us down. One, I retired from the Cronk. And two, the price of crude collapsed, from more than $100 a barrel down into the 20-somethings. Ouch.

We're a long way from the poor house, but suddenly maintaining the apartment in an expensive high-rise in Houston and keeping the country place here at Winedale—well, this has become a big dose to swallow. Right now we're both tapping our savings, our capital, to pay living expenses, and that has to cease pretty soon. Or we'll need to sell either Winedale or Inwood Manor.

All this is why I stopped writing the journal. Instead, I went back to work. No, not at the Chronicle. At the tender age of 94, I'm trying to get into the freelance market, sell a few pieces to magazines. So far, I haven't even submitted anything. I'm having a hard time writing a piece I'd want to submit.

I look back over my shoulder, at those 60-odd years I kept the column going and wrote eleven books and sometimes held down moonlight jobs to pay the bills and I marvel that I ever did it. It was hard. I didn't realize how hard it was when it was going on. And I'm having a tough time getting it going again.

10 AUGUST

I'm pleased to get back to the journal at last. Long time since the last entry, and here's why:

Taking a close look at our financial position, we discovered that we were spending more money than we were taking in, so we decided that we better cut back, which we did, considerably.

Two things had happened almost at the same time, and they pretty well shot us down. One, I retired from the Cronk. And two, the price of crude collapsed, from more than $100 a barrel down into the twenty-somethings. Ouch.

Maybe I could go back to work, I thought. No, not at the *Chronicle*. Try the freelance market, sell a few pieces to magazines. So far, though, I haven't submitted anything. I'm having a hard time writing a piece I'd want to submit.

I look back over my shoulder, at those sixty-odd years I kept the column going and wrote eleven books and sometimes held down moonlight jobs to pay the bills and I marvel that I ever did it. It was hard. I didn't realize how hard it was when it was going on.

On a happier note, I'm sitting now in what we've come to call My Office, which is the glassed-in half of the front porch. A minute ago my side vision caught a movement down in the flowerbed, about five feet from my chair. It was a roadrunner, which has stopped now, and is looking at me through the glass wall.

I think it's a hen. She appears curious, puzzled. As if she's asking, "What is this huge hunk of Something, staring down at me? Is it harmless? Is it dangerous?"

I reach for my cell phone, hoping to get a photo of this visitor. But the movement sends the roadrunner scooting on its way, apparently convinced that I'm something to fear.

We love roadrunners. So do rural Mexicans. In Mexico this fine bird is called Paisano (fellow countryman) and having it run along beside a traveler is considered good fortune.

In my growing-up time in Eastland and on Grandma Hale's place we called the bird a *chapparal*. In fact, I don't believe the roadrunner name was in wide use until those cartoons began showing up in the newspapers and at theaters. *Chapparal* is the Spanish word for brush, or thicket, with native bushes and low-growing trees.

A pair of these birds has raised a couple of offspring not far from this house. We've seen them crossing the road when we drive to Round Top.

The sight of roadrunners always brings up early memories of my father, from the time we lived out there in the little gip-water towns of Hamlin and Stamford. This was in the mid-1920s. I was pre-school age, 4 or 5. (I have to call him "my father" even in this journal. I think we've already dealt with why I can't refer to him as "Daddy.")

That poor man had a merciless work schedule. I have few recollections of spending time with him as a pre-schooler. But those few are precious to me because at that time I counted him the greatest of all men.

I see him planting the flag in the sidewalk in front of the dry goods store where he worked. I see him rolling up to our house and tossing me a new baseball from his open driver-side window, before the car stopped moving.

And I see him firing a twenty-two rifle from that same window of that same car. He is shooting prairie dogs, and I am in the front seat beside him, looking over his shoulder. This had to be a

Sunday afternoon when the store was closed because it was open day and night at all other times.

I'm not sure why seeing the roadrunner generates this memory. I don't recall seeing roadrunners with my father, but maybe I did.

He liked guns. And loved horses, and he was a good rider. When we visited Grandma's farm he'd ride bareback, and put me on the horse behind him. I had to be three or four then, before we moved west from Stephenville. There's a day in my memory bank when he rode out, with me behind him, and he held a sawed-off shotgun in his right hand.

How a sawed-off shotgun ever came to be part of the armament at Grandma's I can only guess. It would not have belonged to my father. He owned a target rifle but never a shotgun. Probably it belonged to one of his brothers. But it was such a curiosity that the family talked about it, and I remember it, the blue of the barrel, and the men holding it out with one hand and firing it like a pistol.

My father fired it off a horse, on this day I'm remembering, while I sat behind him clutching his belt with both hands. I did love riding with him that way. Sometimes I would bury my face in the back of his shirt, and smell him, and think that I was a lucky kid to have a father who could do these wonderful things.

26 SEPTEMBER

A hundred years from now, if the planet survives until then, political historians will still be writing about the bizarre 2016 presidential campaign. Hillary Clinton vs. Donald Trump. It was just plain nasty.

So now here we are on the big day, when the candidates have their first debate. I've never seen Babette so nervous. She's truly concerned that Trump will be our next president. If that comes to pass, I agree the entire planet will be in deep trouble.

But I don't believe it'll happen. If Hillary handles Trump in the debates the way I think she will, I think she'll move along and win the election.

27 SEPTEMBER

OK, no problem. Hillary was a rock in the first debate. And Trump came across, to me, as a blustering fool.

29 SEPTEMBER

We're now in the middle of the semi-annual antiques show in neighboring Fayette County. Antiques. Most of what I see displayed along Highway 237 wouldn't qualify as antiques. Collectibles, maybe. Local folks commonly referred to it as junk.

But then one person's junk is another's treasure. It happens that I'm in the market this year for a mule shoe, an old and rusty one to be nailed over the door of the scooter shed here at Winedale. For purposes of good luck. This shed was built by our friend Richard Hornberger to house Babette's four-wheel scooter, which she rides when walking the dog in the woods. So she really scoots the dog, instead of walking it.

We have two outbuildings at Winedale, a small barn and this scooter shed. The barn is properly equipped with a mule shoe but the scooter shed lacks this improvement. It's a state law, sort of, that mule shoes must be nailed above the doors of barns and sheds and other outbuildings.

But personally I don't do the mule shoe thing because I'm superstitious. I'm like my father on superstition. He always said he'd never be superstitious in any way because it's bad luck.

When city slickers come out in the country and buy property and pretend to be ranchers and farmers, they often acquire items of ancient farm equipment and put them on display. Like rusty plows, or cultivators. Sometimes even a lug-wheeled tractor that hasn't moved under its own power since 1922.

We haven't decorated Winedale much. Most of what we have was here when we bought the place. An old water well pulley. A homemade dinner bell, triangular-shaped, with a metal wand to make it ring and call the hands to dinner from the field. A rusty cow bell. These are hanging on the front porch. No, that metal thing hanging between the cow bell and the pulley is not a relic. It's a dog poop picker upper.

Maybe I need to get with the game and acquire a few more relics. Our neighbor to the north, Randon Dillingham, has an antique fire truck. It still runs and comes complete with a siren which Randy cranks up on the Fourth of July and scares hell out of all the wild life.

30 SEPTEMBER

Wait, I forgot to mention my churn, with wooden dasher, which occupies a place of honor on the front porch. Crock churns like this are still for sale but I didn't know that, and when I saw one on display I snapped it up as if it were the last one on the planet. My intention was to buy two or three gallons of fresh milk, right out of the cow, let it sit and clabber, and see if I could make a pound of butter.

Babette has never seen this process, and she's recognized as an educated person. How can a woman be fully educated if she's never seen anybody churn?

Every time I walk out of this old house in the morning that churn greets me, and takes me back to Mulberry Street in Eastland. There I sit on the back porch in my bib overalls, working the churn dasher up and down, up and down.

Then my mother appears, pulls the dasher up enough to look in and see if the butter is coming yet. If not, she goes back in the kitchen for a cup of cold water and pours this in the churn. Cold water added that way makes the butter come quicker. Why? Don't ask me. All I know is, that's the way my mother did it.

When the butter came, as the saying was, it rose to the top of the liquid, which then had become buttermilk. My part in the process was finished at this point. What came now was beyond the capability of an amateur, or anyway it was at our house. My mother took over, and separated the butter from the buttermilk and worked it into a butter mold.

This wooden butter mold, washed so many hundreds of times, always struck me as the cleanest object we owned.

Well, maybe the wooden stick used to punch the boiling clothes in the wash pot deserved at least a tie for cleanliness. That implement was immersed in soapy, boiling water so often it was almost white. I once got a serious scolding for trying to kill a grasshopper with our wash pot stick.

1 OCTOBER

Before we leave country relics: I've failed to mention that we have a small rusty iron water pump sitting on the front porch. It's less than two feet tall, with a nice long handle. Kind of pump once used on shallow water wells.

Early in the 1930s—I don't remember the year—we moved to Glen Rose when the Great Depression was going strong. Why Glen Rose? Beats me. Probably because my father had found us a place to live close to rent free, and we could spade up a garden and raise vegetables.

The house was out on the edge of town where municipal luxuries such as running water had not yet arrived. There was a shallow well in the back yard rigged with a hand pump like this one here at Winedale. All our water—for drinking, cooking, bathing—came out of that well, via the hand pump. I personally pumped hundreds of bucketsful. Pumping water was one of my chores.

In the '70s when I was running around the state doing stories for The Houston Post, I finally got back to Glen Rose and I thought about that pump. Could it possibly be there yet, and working?

The house was still standing, although it had been renovated and duded up with new paint. I almost failed to recognize it. I knocked on the door and this mid-aged woman opened up, looking unfriendly. Before I could wish her a pleasant afternoon she said she didn't want anything.

This didn't discourage me because in that job I had already knocked on dozens of doors and been mistaken for a salesman many times.

Before the woman could shut the door I backed off three or four steps, to show I didn't intend to charge in and murder her. And quickly I launched into my little I'm-not-selling-anything speech, winding up with "the only reason I knocked on your door, I'm interested in the water well in your back yard."

She said, "What're you talkin' about?"

Which was her question, so she had to give me time to answer. I told her about living in that house with my family during the Depression, and pumping water from the well about twenty feet from her back door.

She was shaking her head. "No, you've got the wrong house. Never was any water well in the yard of this place."

I said I'd be grateful if she'd just let me look at the spot where I thought the well was. Wouldn't take but a couple of minutes. Her response was silent but I read it loud and clear: "I don't let strangers in my house." I told her I didn't need to come through the house, I'd just walk around.

I knew I had the right house, even though the twisted cedar in the side yard was three times bigger than I remembered. I'd nailed a small bird house in that cedar when I was eight years old, and wrens had built in it, and hatched their babies.

My hostess was already standing at the back door when I came around from the front. That yard, when we lived there, was hard bare ground. Sometimes we swept it, like people in the country did. But now it was covered in thick St. Augustine sod.

Even so, I walked straight to the spot where the well was, got down on one knee, parted the grass with both hands to reveal a metal plate that capped the old well. I asked the woman if she'd take a look.

She walked out to peer at the cap and said, "Well I'll swan."

I'm still not certain why finding that old well site pleased me so much, but the discovery remains truly important to me. It's almost as if that small disk, hidden in the grass, is a marker, a memorial to those strange times we lived in.

2 OCTOBER

I still have some decorating to do in my Winedale office, which we formed by glassing off half of the front porch. I do have a few items displayed on the inside wall.

One is a plaque commemorating Apollo 11, the space shot that put the first man on the moon, in 1969. I consider our space exploration to be the biggest news story of my life. Not that I had anything to do with it, other than to be a cheer leader for the program. It needed cheer leaders, and still does.

Of the seven original astronauts, I met two of them, shook their hands, visited briefly. One was Deke Slaton, whom I met in a bar at Canaveral when I went down there hoping to watch a space shot. (The count-down went all the way to four, three, two—and shut down before lift-off. I made two more trips back to Canaveral but never got to see a launch.)

The other original astronaut I met was Alan Shepard. It happened in Buffalo Hardware in Houston, where we were both buying kitchen garbage cans.

Gene Cernan—not one of the originals but he was the last man on the moon—I sat by him at a concert. Nice guy. He talked about the pleasure he still got from flying. In a spacecraft? No, in a little single-engine tail dragger.

All those astronauts were true heroes to me, especially the early ones.

Also on my office wall is a fine rusty mule shoe I picked up in a pasture just outside Chappell Hill. I brought it back to Houston and glued it to a piece of cardboard. Inside the U of the shoe I wrote in box car letters, "GOOD LUCK TO ME." And added the date, "Aug 3, 1980."

At that time I was feeling in serious need of good fortune. In April of '80 I had left Pasadena, and gone through my second divorce in the previous five years. I had managed to make two wives unhappy, and I wasn't singing any joyful songs myself.

Those two divorces thoroughly cleaned my plow. I was practically on the street, staying temporarily in Liz Bennett's apartment while Liz was on an extended trip into Mexico. While there I began writing, on the mule shoe's cardboard, the dates of significant events in my recent history. When I left Bryan. When I married Ellen Belle[1]. When I left Pasadena. When I moved into Liz's apartment. When this happened. When that happened.

I've continued to do that, and the mule shoe is with me yet, nailed to the office wall here at the Winedale place. It shows the dates of when I moved into Treetops Apartments. When I met Babette. When I left the *Post* and went over to the Cronk. When Babette and I married. When I moved to Stanmore. When we rented Winedale. When we bought Winedale.

---

1. Ellen Belle Mabry

Most of the important dates of my life are recorded on this small square of cardboard with a mule shoe attached. My favorite date written there is when I met Babette, in 1981. That's when everything began looking up for me. Sometimes I wonder how my life would have gone, if I'd never met her. Probably I'd have died in my 70s, because I wasn't behaving any too well. Instead, I was given a monstrous party on my 90th birthday (courtesy guess who), and five years later I'm still here to tell about it.

The prettiest decoration here in the Winedale office is a picture of my girl, who smiles at me from a shelf of books. Not far from her beautiful face is a blue bird nest with three eggs in it. I found the nest here in the yard, abandoned, probably because of threats from a chicken snake or a coon or a pair of jaybirds.

Then over yonder by the door, held on the wall by a few second-hand nails, is my branding iron. When heated and applied to a surface it'll produce my brand—LH connected. It was made and given to me by my pilot friend, Joe Matlock of Victoria.

This is a genuine branding iron, registered in Victoria County and every bit as legal as the running W of the King Ranch or the XIT or any other famous Texas brand. I've heated it and applied it often but never to the hip of a calf or to anything that could feel the burn. After I'm gone, visitors to Winedale will find my LH connected stamped on various wooden surfaces on our sprawling 10-acre ranch.

Before we were married I put my brand on Babette, but I must not tell you where. I used a Marks-a-Lot.

I could mention my wall decoration that came from Europe. Because one of these times, long after I'm history, relatives of mine not yet born might be in this office looking at the strange stuff the old man had on his walls. And they'll wonder about the scale.

In the early 1990s Babette and I were spending a month in France, down in that Dordogne River country. We rented a place to stay in the little village of Tremolat.

One morning we were out walking when local farmers and gardeners were selling vegetables in the middle of town, so we bought a few. Green beans. Onions. Two or three potatoes. The lady selling these veggies used a small rusty scale, about a foot long, to weigh them and calculate prices. I was interested in the scale because it was, in miniature, almost exactly like a Texas cotton scale, with the single metal beam and the pea-weight. I wanted that scale, and offered to buy it from the gardener but she said oh no, she couldn't do without it.

Back at the house I told our landlord (what was his name, Andre? I think it was Andre) about my interest in the little scale. He went home and returned with a rusty scale exactly like the one used by the gardener, and said he'd be pleased if I'd accept it as a gift.

So that's why I now have a French garden scale on my wall here at Winedale. Who knows how old it is. It looks primitive, ancient. I think it's beautiful.

Babette's making migas for supper. She's expert at migas.

6 OCTOBER

Hey, the first week of October has given us some nice honest weather. We're grateful, because in the last few years October has been double-crossing us with its 90-degree highs and 78-degree lows.

Remind me to go out and pour a gallon of Clorox in our septic system. This is a little chore I do the first week of every month. I forget what favorable function this chemical performs but the plumbers say the system needs it so I keep buying the stuff and pouring it in the hole where they tell me to pour it. My father raised me to believe everything a plumber says. His policy was, Never mind doctors and lawyers but don't doubt a plumber.

The gentle breeze is harvesting acorns from our oaks. They produce a loud bang, roll-roll-roll, when they hit the tin roof just over my head. I like this.

10 OCTOBER

October has taken up its wicked ways again, punishing us with 90-degree days and no rain.

We are gearing up for a visit from Will and Declan Warren. Will is forty-two and his son Declan is four. They live in New York City in a tall building. Here at Winedale Will was exposed to rural life when he was young but it didn't do him any permanent damage. He is now the vice president of something very important. It has to do with the Future so I don't try to understand it.

Declan is a handsome, intelligent kid, the smartest four-year-old I've ever met. Will wants him to visit Winedale. Why not? The kid could own this place someday, if it stays in the family. I suspect Decky is too young right now to enjoy our vast acreage, but I'm not consulted on such matters.

Will and I have always gotten along well and I'll be pleased to see him. He and Decky are due to fly in on the 13th and return to New York on the 16th. Stand by.

18 OCTOBER

OK, we've had the visit and it went fairly well, I think. What the four-year-old New Yorker enjoyed most about rural living was the cartoons on the television, the same shows he watches in that tall building in Manhattan.

Will wanted him exposed to catching a fish so I rigged up an old rod and reel with mono line and a light sinker and a red and white plastic bobber. We bought a little carton of night crawlers at Merc in Round Top (I don't dig worms anymore), and went down to the tank.

Three years ago this small stock tank was choked with aquatic vegetation (moss, we call it) so I financed a tubful of tilapia fingerlings and dumped 'em in there. Tilapia are said to be vegetarians that will eat this moss, and they did. In fact, they cleared every last bite of greenery out of the tank, and its water is now quite low and showing a sicky green cast.

I had no idea we'd catch anything, using earthworms for bait to attract a vegetarian fish. Will said don't worry, we didn't need to catch anything, he just wanted his son to have the experience of going fishing. But our first worm was hardly wet before we hooked a nice eating-size tilapia, maybe three-quarters of a pound. Put up such a fight on that light tackle, it managed to frighten the boy and he backed away from the action.

Will went ahead and fished and caught half a dozen more tilapia about the same size so the effort was a considerable success.

I don't believe the four-year-old was much entertained by the fish-catching. However, I may have impressed him by getting my feet tangled up and falling on my butt and rolling down the tank dam and almost into the water. Didn't hurt me. I've become experienced at falling since I got into my nineties, and I expect the sight of me going down that tank dam was a lot more interesting than trying to catch a vegetarian fish.

While they were here, my granddaughter Kacy Hale put on a long white dress and pulled off her shoes and got married barefooted on a beach in Florida. Her last name is now Hoefler, or something similar.

Kacy was born and raised in Kansas, a long way from any ocean, but she was exposed to beaches at an early age and has been drawn toward salt water ever since. Evidently this is a habit that present-day brides have acquired. That is, they go a long, long way from home and find a place to get married, requiring family and friends to spend themselves into bankruptcy just to attend the wedding.

Me, I wouldn't travel all the way to Florida to watch Melania Trump get married naked to Bill Clinton. Besides, we had company.

Kacy is a dear girl and we love her. She is a surgical nurse, pure bred and registered, and I'm pleased to say I wrote a few checks to help her through all that wicked training.

I also wrote a few checks to help push her brother Travis through college. A few to help her father through, as well. A few more to help my grandson Daniel through. And of those four, Kacy is the only one that didn't quit before graduation. I wish now I'd have taken all the thousands I spent on the three who quit and used it to send Becky to the best university we could afford. Or, if she refused to go, I could have bought the Mercedes I always wanted, instead of driving a Ford all these years.

Back to the wedding on the beach. On Facebook we have a video of Mark dancing with the bride. I didn't know he could dance but then I've been acquainted with him only sixty-five years. I can't tell from these wedding pictures whether he's wearing shoes but I see he's got on a necktie. I bet he flung it in the Gulf when the wedding was over.

Kacy's new husband is a nice looking young man. I don't know if he can talk, though. I've met him a time or two but never heard him make a sound.

Back in Kansas and on nursing duty at the hospital, Kacy reports that they're working her hard since she took several days off to get married. Her first day she put in twelve hours and did three gall bladders, two appendectomies and a foot.

7 NOVEMBER

Election Eve. Hillary Clinton vs. Donald Trump.

Babette and I have already voted, via U.S. Mail, so we're here at Winedale waiting for the result. Our legal address is still Houston so that's where we vote. A record number of Houstonians have voted early as we did but thousands and thousands stood in line, many in the rain, to avoid even longer lines tomorrow.

I think and hope that all this eagerness by voters means a big win for Hillary but the fact is I'm a little nervous that it'll go the other way. I don't believe it will, and yet I wouldn't bet the farm against Trump. Strange, that such a creature is actually running for president.

Here in the country we're sitting on the border between Washington and Fayette counties and they always go solidly Republican in any kind of election. So I'm really interested to see whether they go for Trump.

I personally have heard zero political talk around here. Nobody at the Post Office or the grocery store has asked me to vote one way or the other. I haven't even overheard anybody else talking about how they might vote. In Round Top I've seen only two Trump Pence yard signs, and no Hillary signs at all.

Books, a library of them, will be written some day about this bizarre campaign.

9 NOVEMBER

Well, Trump won and I can't stand even to say anything beyond that. Heaven help us, Trump *won*.

11 NOVEMBER

Along with many of our friends we're going through a period of grief. About the election, yes. We feel that our country has just suffered a disaster, a pure tragedy, with the election of Trump.

15 NOVEMBER

We've had our first book signing of the year at that second-hand store in Houston, the name of which I seldom remember. It went about like we expected. Not so good. We may be making a mistake, scheduling autographings without a new book to offer.

A year ago our little "One Man's Christmas" did so well that several shops, including a couple of B&N's, asked for autographings this year. I'm not entirely comfortable with the plan. We'll see, when we get closer to Christmas, how it goes.

22 NOVEMBER

This Trump thing has thrown a wet blanket over everything Babette and I enjoy. I can't get rid of the feeling that we have chosen The Enemy to lead the nation. This guy represents everything I'm against.

His election may have changed, permanently, how I feel about the future of this country. Never before, since I cast my first vote, have I lost confidence in the judgment and common sense of the American people. I've always thought that, in chorus, we often swing too far to the left, or too far to the right, but before we go over the cliff we come to our senses and swing back toward the middle and somehow end up doing what we need to do, or almost. I loved that system. I thought it was the American way.

But this time I'm afraid the system has allowed us to make The Big Mistake. I don't believe that all those who voted for Trump are bad people but I do believe a great many of them were ill informed, and didn't understand what they were doing. They wanted change, but with Trump I doubt they'll ever get the kind of change they voted for.

Babette, who knows political history (at least 40 times more of it than I do) can deliver a chilling rant about the way Trump operates, and how similar it is to that of Hitler and the Nazis.

THANKSGIVING DAY

Our birds have disappeared. All of them, even the crows and damn near all the buzzards. I put seed on the feeders and the coons come at night and clean it up. It's like they eat the birds, too, because there ain't nuthin left around here with feathers on it.

Audubon (I've been trying for 50 years to learn how that word is spelled) says don't worry, the birds have abandoned feeders because of heavy rains last spring. All that moisture produced tons of grass and brush in fields and woods and those plants are now heading out and providing plenty of food for birds. These avian experts say the birds will be back at our feeders soon. Maybe so.

15 DECEMBER

We're in Houston for a few days. Usual reasons. Dentist. Doctors. And a few book signings. Had a visit with Becky. She's excited about next year because she's signed up with some of her bridge-playing friends to go to Africa in the fall. This is the big trip—four weeks, safari-style, see all the animals on migration.

Mark still working the golf courses. Doing all right. Can you believe both my children are into their sixties?

Attended a meeting of unit owners in our high-rise, Inwood Manor. The building is in process of being renovated and this is causing hardship for some residents. One example, at some point in the next year, everybody will be obliged to move out and live somewhere else for a week or ten days because there'll be no water and no power in the building.

We're fortunate to have the Winedale place, where we can live in reasonable comfort while all that Houston construction is going on.

20 DECEMBER

Four days after Christmas. I've been neglecting this journal in recent weeks, I think mainly because I'm feeling so low about the future. Trump continues to scare half the country out of its skin with his idiotic Tweets and his cabinet nominations. The idea that this crazy person, starting next January 20th, will have his finger on the nuclear switch—well, it does disturb sleep.

A minute ago: A huge bird, one of the hawks that spend the winter in this part of the world, gave me a little show. It came sailing from our front gate, maybe two feet off the ground, on a heading exactly toward me, sitting here in my office chair behind a glass wall. Bird's wings were fully spread, probably six feet wide and held level for maximum speed.

I had time enough to think, Hey, if this creature maintains its heading and velocity, it could crash into my glass window and right into my lap.

But hawks are not that stupid. Maybe twenty feet from the yard fence, the bird threw its wings open to perform a remarkable braking maneuver. Its body rose ten feet, and settled with infinite grace on top of a fence post.

NEW YEAR'S EVE

The last day of what many people are calling a bad year.

Feeling pretty well today. Up at six A.M. Spent forty-five minutes cleaning up the kitchen. Fed the dog. Checked the news to see if Trump did anything stupid that endangered the nation even before he takes office. Drove to Round Top and the Post Office. Stopped at the grocery store. Picked up a gallon of Clorox to pour in the septic system.

Babette still sleeping. Good, because I know she had not gotten to sleep at one-thirty A.M. This is fairly common with her. Some mornings I don't see her until ten o'clock. Other mornings I'll find her in the kitchen drinking tea and playing with the dog at five A.M. She has a really difficult time getting adequate rest. Light sleeper. Hears noises I can't hear even with my hearing aids on and the volume jacked up. Smells things I haven't smelled in twenty years. She has doubtful vision but she sees things I can't see.

New Year's Eve. Will we celebrate? Go out? Maybe. Soon as it turns dark we might go out on the back porch, for five minutes, and watch the fireworks that the neighbors still shoot. If they're not too loud, that is. We don't like loud noises. Then we'll do same thing we do every night—watch TV. At least Babette will watch it. About nine-thirty she'll wake me up and say it's time to go to bed.

2017

My first journal entry of 2017. And isn't this Becky's birthday? I think so. At least it's her natural birthday, on which she receives no gifts because it's so close to Christmas and everybody's already tired buying and giving presents.

When she was in high school, I changed her birthday from January third to something later on in the year, like June 14th or Sepember 10th, and she liked those dates a lot better. I still do this, picking a different date every year.

People say to me, "You can't just change a person's birthday." But you can. I've done it many times.

This year her birthday will be in October because that's when she'll go on that African safari. I'll help her on trip expense and that will be her birthday present.

I well remember the night she was born, sixty-five years ago, because her entry into Texas was so much easier, for me, than her brother's a couple of years earlier. I thought I would surely die when Mark was having such a hard time getting born. He took so long, and I sat by his mama's bed through those endless hours of labor and that's when I decided that I was opposed to the way babies are born.

I still am. It's nothing but cruel. Why should a woman have to endure torture to become a mother? Having a child is the most extraordinary of all human experience. It's downright miraculous, and needs to be gentle, and exalting. There should be joyful music, and angels singing. Not pain, not suffering.

When we went to the hospital for Becky's birth, after we got Helen checked in she told me to leave, go somewhere else, that she didn't need me to sit there and share every pain.

Did I go? You bet I did. I was so grateful to her for that release and I still am.

Even now, I can't stay in the room when a birth is being televised, and TV is flat in love with labor scenes and birth scenes. When one comes on, I go to the kitchen and check to see if there's any ice cream left in the freezer.

5 JANUARY

We're getting some winter weather here at Winedale and that's good. Already had one solid freeze and another forecast for tonight.

This old house withstands freezing weather better than I thought it would when we moved into it. We've got the pipes and faucets wrapped and stone skirting all around the place. We've had temps down into the teens and no busted plumbing. Not yet anyway. Knock-knock.

A big pot of vegetable stew for supper. Vegetable stew may sound mild, even weak, but when Babette gets through stirring in all the spices, it'll make you want to become a card-carrying vegetarian.

6 JANUARY

Just finished reading about plans for the presidential inauguration, coming up January 20th. Obama and Michelle will attend, and Bill and Hillary and George and Laura (but not Papa Bush because he's almost old as I am and not too frisky) and even Jimmy Carter says count me in.

I am feeling absolutely nauseated that a creature like Donald Trump is about to become the president of my country. I cringe at the thought of it. I vomit on the fact of it.

Imagine for one paragraph that an angel appeared to me and said, "I have a deal for you, offered by the Lord. He can change the result of the recent election, so that Hillary will be president instead of Donald Trump. But God demands a price. You must give up whatever remains of your life. Say yes, and on January 20 Hillary will move into the White House, Trump will go to Florida forever, and you will be a goner. What say you?"

I say, "Yes, it's a deal."

So I hear you laughing, saying, "Yeah but you're not giving up much. At ninety-five? And in doubtful health? What if the same deal were offered when you were thirty-five? Would you have said yes then?"

Maybe not, but I disagree that I wouldn't be giving up much at ninety-five. Whatever I have left—a year or three years or six months—is precious to me. But I would give it up to keep this creature out of the Oval Office because I think he will lead my country into disaster.

7 JANUARY

At seven A.M. this morning my feed store thermometer on the front porch said the temp was nineteen degrees. I was relieved that water flowed freely from the kitchen tap.

Today at three-thirty P.M. in Houston our Texans play (I forget who) in the first game of the NFL playoffs. They're 9-7 on the season and damned if I know how they ever made the play-offs. My prediction is that they'll get whipped.

They've got this new quarterback who stands something like six-feet-eight-inches and can throw a football seventy yards but he's always completing passes to players who aren't on our side.

Hey, we've been invited to a dinner party, at the home of our new neighbors Stan and Melanie Mays. I hear the main dish will be chili. Be interesting to see what Melanie and Stan consider to be chili. A lot of different dishes answer to that name in this state.

A chili party reminds me of the first World Championship Chili Cookoff held out at Terlingua. I was there, sure. What year was that—1967 or '68?

This event came about because the writer H. Allen Smith challenged Wick Fowler to a chili-making match.

Smith at the time was a nationally known writer. Did books like "Low Man on a Totem Pole," and "Life in a Putty Knife Factory."

Fowler was a writer for *The Dallas News* who had gained notoriety writing about chili. He established a business with his 2-Alarm Chili Mix, a good product still sold in grocery stores.

That first chili match drew planet-wide attention, and gave Fowler a super-valuable boost to his chili mix business. The match ended in a tie because the competition was a shameless sham. Smith's chili recipe was polluted with stuff like green bell peppers and other ingredients totally foreign to genuine chili.

Smith ended up buying a place out there in the Big Bend Country and got acquainted with Old Friend Morgan. Morgan at the time was running that mining operation for Dow, just across the Rio. I used to go out there and stay with him and do border stories for the paper.

Apparently Morgan and H. Allen had a smooth friendship going for a while. Morgan was good about helping writers of all kinds who wandered into that part of the world. But his relationship with Smith struck a stump when, according to Morgan, Smith stole one of my stories.

I had done a yarn out there on how a Mexican lottery works. (The last name drawn out of the hat wins the prize, instead of the first.) Apparently Smith took a clipping of my lottery piece, rewrote it and sold it as his own. At least that's the story Morgan told me, and it really pissed him off. It didn't bother me because I never saw what Smith wrote, and for all I know he got his information for the lottery story from the same source I did. From Morgan, that is.

8 JANUARY

Melanie's chili turned out to be good, and we met a few nice folks at her party. One is a native German who told a long story about how he, with his family, barely escaped the Nazis in WWII.

I didn't get to tell a story. I intended to tell one about covering that first chili cook-off at Terlingua. Figured it would be appropriate since we were attending a chili party. But all the chili talk was about that silly argument on whether beans should be an ingredient in chili and I'm sick of that one.

A lady at the gathering lived her childhood on the 4600 block of Valerie in Bellaire. So probably her family was a neighbor of ours back when Becky was born in 1952. Helen and I built a house in that block, at 4631, in 1950.

We lived there until 1955 when the West Loop was built and the feeder ran through our living room. That house was moved and set up somewhere on west. I tried a couple of times to find where it ended up but never had any success. It was a good house. Its cost was $11,450 and the monthly mortgage payment was seventy-eight dollars and change.

In 1950 I was making something like $375 a month at the *Post* and doing a farm radio program at KPRC five mornings a week. I'd get up at five A.M. Monday through Friday and drive to the Lamar Hotel where KPRC had its studio. Those were tough days.

From the house in Bellaire I'd drive in on Post Oak Road, turn right on Westheimer all the way to Kirby, through River Oaks on Kirby and then Allen Parkway on into downtown.

If I had time I'd slip into One's-a-Meal there on Main. Get

juice and a doughnut and a cup of coffee. Trot across the street
to the Lamar. Ride the elevator to the studio on the mezzanine.
Always short of time. Many a morning I plopped into my chair
and reached for a microphone just as the announcer was intro-
ducing me.

On the program, aimed at farmers and ranchers, I'd do the
weather and the markets (livestock, that is) and any info I thought
would interest country folks. Much of it came from my daily column in the *Post*.

For this curious duty I was paid a "talent fee" of something like
$100 a month. Not much, but it was a gift from heaven because
it paid the mortgage on the house and the light and water and
gas bills.

From that house in Bellaire, we moved to Bryan in 1955. I have
wondered, so many times, what my life would have been like if
we'd remained in Houston. I'm pretty sure Helen and I wouldn't
have stayed married very much longer. (Helen's unhappiness in
Houston was the main reason for the move to Bryan.)

Let's play what-if. What if I'd been cut loose in Houston, a
bachelor, at maybe thirty-two? Hey, I might have met Babette
before she ever married David[1]. Now that's something worth
thinking about. It could have happened. We were in the same
part of town. I know, when I was thirty-two she was only nine or
ten years old, but when she was twenty I was in my early forties
and she's always shown an interest in men a good deal older than
she, isn't that right?

I've decided that I *would* have met her. Of course. It happened.
I remember it now. I was making this talk, and she showed up
in the audience. Sat in the first row. Knock-down beautiful, in a
short skirt and that sexy hair streaming down, and afterward she

---

1. David B. Warren

came up and said the same things she said in that letter she wrote me, about wanting to hear a rural Texan voice, so I took her to Blackie's place and everybody knows the rest of the story. Sometimes I entertain fantasies about being with Babette when I was in my thirties and forties. Hoo boy.

But back to Bellaire.

The first two years of Becky's life were probably the toughest, physically, I've ever spent, and Becky had nothing to do with the difficulty. In fact, Becky was a good baby. Caused little trouble.

The problem was, I had minimum time to rest. My main trouble was caused by Mrs. Hobby[2], who had discovered agriculture and soil conservation along about this time and she decided her newspaper ought to be the foremost journal of the nation in that field. She once summoned me out to the Hobby Mansion off South Main to discuss the matter, how she wanted "the farmers of Texas to set their clocks" by what I wrote in the *Post*.

I had no idea how I was going to do whatever she wanted me to do but I sat there in that great house, in my wrinkled khakis and GI shoes, and kept saying, "yes, ma'am, yes, ma'am."

My immediate boss at this time was Elbert Turner, the state editor. Mrs. Hobby obviously had delivered the same lecture to Elbert because he set me going over half the state covering anything that smelled like an agricultural story. I clocked tons of overtime.

Understand I was doing six columns a week plus covering all that daily stuff and taking pictures with one of those big old clunky speed graphic cameras. And filling and editing an entire farm page on Sundays. Many days I'd roll back into town from a place like Nacogdoches or Victoria about six P.M. and soup negatives and print pictures and write a story to go with them and I might not get home until ten o'clock.

---

2. Oveta Culp Hobby, owner of *The Houston Post*.

And there Helen would be, in a foul humor because she couldn't get Mark to sleep, or something had gone wrong during the day, like the plumbing, or some damn thing the little neighbor kids had done, and by the time I listened to all the daily disasters I might get to bed by midnight. With the alarm set for five A.M., so I could rush downtown to the radio station and start another day.

Was every day like that? No, not every day, or I wouldn't have lasted six months. But that pattern fit too many of them.

When Becky was born we came to an agreement—Helen would get Becky to sleep at night, and I'd take Mark. Becky turned out to be a good sleeper, and Mark was just unshirted hell, always fighting sleep and having nightmares or the belly ache at midnight or wanting a drink of water at 2 a.m.

This kept me so short on rest I'd catch myself dozing off while driving, and I'd have to pull over on the side of the highway and take a 15-minute nap.

A nap? Not a bad idea, for right now.

29 JANUARY

The world has stopped turning for most of January while it watched a global disaster come to pass—the inauguration of President Donald Trump.

I hope I'm wrong but I can't shed the notion that we've just delivered our country into the hands of the enemy.

The women, at least, seem to agree. They've marched against Trump all over the world. I wonder what the egotistical son of a bitch really thinks about millions of women demonstrating that they're opposed to his presidency. Wouldn't surprise me if he's saying, "Look at all these millions of pussies that have sprung into action, all because of me."

Babette and I drove down on Women's March Day and at least showed the flag. Neither of us can walk far. She because of a bum knee awaiting surgery. Me because of ninety-five years and heart trouble. But we trudged a couple of blocks, and took a lot of pictures, and shed a few tears.

We're having a fairly easy winter. Lot of cool nights and days with highs in the 70s. We've had a couple of good freezes and if we don't get another by the middle of February these weekend farmers around here will proclaim that spring has arrived and start putting out tomato plants.

Then around March 6th or 7th a blizzard will blow in and destroy all the tomatoes. This is a frequent pattern of events that helps the sellers of tomato plants make a living.

30 JANUARY

Monday morning, 11:30 a.m. Stock market is down 182 points (the Dow). Who knows where it'll go if Trump keeps regurgitating stupid presidential orders, as he did on immigration last weekend. About half of what I'm worth is invested in blue chip stocks. Let us pray.

I wish now that I had taken about 10 grand out of my savings five years ago and put it in the market, which has done nothing during Obama's administration but go up. But I didn't do it because the rule says a dude of my age should not be heavily invested in equities. Too risky.

8 FEBRUARY

Here's a letter from one of the customers who is curious about my religion. I've had these religion letters for years, going back into the 1950s when I started doing the column. Some come from evangelists who are afraid I'm going to hell and seem truly worried about me. Most come from those who appear mainly curious.

Like this one that I just now read. Judging, as he says, from reading the column for almost half a century, he has decided that I have respect for the religion that my Methodist mother practiced, but I don't practice it myself. He wants to know if that's true.

If I answer his letter I'll give this fellow the same answer I've given to others. Which is, that the religion I practice (if that's the proper verb) is so purely personal that I'm not comfortable talking about it, so I don't. I ought to add that I at least try to practice it. My record shows I'm a long way from perfect. That's all I care to say, to anybody, about my religion.

VALENTINE'S DAY

The stock market had that little drop right after the inauguration but since then it has continued a small but steady climb. Here in the humming industrial center of Winedale we are in favor of a rising market but I have mixed feelings about it. A rising market tends to make more Americans say. "Well, maybe Trump's not so bad. Maybe he'll be all right."

I am not one of those Americans thinking any such thing.

On this dark, wet Valentine's Day, I salute *New York Times* columnist Thomas Friedman who wrote a piece shouting out his belief that this country needs desperately to find out what is going on between Trump and Russia. Hear, hear. Something is stinking about that question, and we're just lolly-gagging along as if everything is all right.

19 FEBRUARY

For Valentine's I brought Babette a dozen supermarket roses from HEB in Brenham. They cost thirteen dollars so you know these were the highest class of rose. They were at least the highest class being sold at HEB, there among the cucumbers and roasting ears.

But Babette said their color was especially deep and rich, and she kept them in the house long past the time they began turning up their toes and shedding.

3 MARCH

The month of March came in with a great roaring noise, made by the bulldozers and excavators and trucks of one Ronnie Jahntz, professional earth mover. Ronnie and his machinery are here and stirring dirt to repair the great hole last summer's 20-inch rain dug in the spillway of our tank.

That hole was impressive. Maybe eight feet deep and ten in diameter. We had it fenced off to keep dogs and deer and wandering humans from falling in.

I confess: I do like to watch a skilled dozer operator touch a small lever and move a mountain of soil.

So the great hole is now filled and Ronnie has shaped out a new, wider spillway and Babette doesn't like the look of it and neither do I. It needs smoothing. But guys who move dirt with dozers aren't totally dedicated to smooth. Somebody else must come along and do the smoothing.

4 MARCH

Ever since I began this journal I've debated off and on whether I ought to include an account of my departure from Bryan. I think

I'll try it. If the journal pretends to be about my life, then my leaving Bryan needs to be part of the story because that chapter covers the most extraordinary thing I ever did.

Not the worst thing. Not the best thing. But the most extraordinary, because it was something I thought I would never do. I considered myself incapable of it. (Just for the record, I'll say before I begin that I'm glad I did it, and that it was, in various ways, the right thing to do.)

When Mark and Becky were growing up, Helen and I. . . well, we managed. We worked at it, and kept the marriage afloat. Plowed through some rough times.

I had many days when I told myself I ought to pack up and leave. Yeah, but where would I go? To Houston? And live alone in an apartment? And abandon those two kids?

(Actually, during the worst of the domestic upheavals with the kids still at home, I did leave, for brief periods. But guilt soon pushed me right on back.)

Fast forward to the fall of 1974. Kids are gone. Mark was in Florida, playing ball. Becky was working and living in Austin. And things at home were worse instead of better.

During the summer of '74, in the midst of this unhappiness, I met Ellen Belle. Wrote a column about her. She was an artist, a piano player, a widow living alone in Pasadena. I thought she was everything Helen was not. She read books, sang songs, spoke Spanish, had travelled widely, loved music and dogs and art. And she invited me to come live with her.

Was I in love with her? No, but I thought I was. I think now that what I was in love with was her invitation. Here was my ticket out of Bryan. I could now leave with a destination, and one that looked pretty damned good. A widow of just about the right age, and a pretty one, at that, and she's got a nice home with a grandfather clock and a baby grand piano in the living room and a swimming pool in the back yard.

Despite all that, leaving wasn't easy. Sure, I knew what I ought to do. I composed the speech, practiced it. The one that begins, "I hate to say this but I'm leaving you, and I want a divorce. . . "

Even when I practiced, I couldn't get the words to come out. Breaking up a marriage the right way, if there is a right way, was simply impossible for me. So I decided to go ahead and do it the wrong way. I would just run off.

That wasn't easy, either. I wrote what I called The Flight Plan, all the details necessary to get away when Helen was not in the house. I worked on the plan for weeks. I needed careful preparation because Helen had become close to a recluse. She almost never left the house alone.

One exception: Every Tuesday, due to a non-operative washing machine in our garage, she loaded two laundry baskets of soiled clothes in the old '52 Merc we were using for a family car, and went to the Washateria a half mile from the house.

I clocked her for a month. On average she needed a little less than two hours to wash, dry and fold the laundry and drive back home. This told me how much time I had to load my car and get away before she returned. So I planned, and rehearsed. I isolated the work materials I'd need. Typewriter, copy paper, carbons, books, etc. out of my home office. Placed them in a stack that I could pick up quickly and carry out.

In that same way I arranged everything else I intended to take. Clothes, for instance. I took only one armload of clothes but these had to be hung in a casual pattern in the closet, so they wouldn't look Prepared. And yet they had to be hung so that I could reach in and scoop them up on one arm.

I decided in advance that I needed an hour to load and leave the house. I practiced, going through dry runs until I cut my time down to forty-five minutes.

The weekend before I planned to depart on the following Tuesday, we went up to Camp Creek Lake where we had the fishing cabin. That place had a wooden pier, similar to the one on our Winedale tank. Planks on its deck had rotted and I spent most of that weekend replacing those boards.

I did a pretty good job of it. When I finished I walked up the path to the cabin and turned and looked at the pier, and the boathouse, and all the stuff I'd worked on for fifteen years. I'd put a lot of myself into that place, so I gave it a slow goodbye. I figured I'd never see it again, and I have not.

Did H. suspect anything? I think so. The Tuesday morning I was to leave, I was so nervous I could hardly drink a cup of coffee. She asked, "What's wrong with you?" I said, "Nothing."

When she backed out, I didn't start my loading immediately. I waited 10 minutes and followed her, to make certain she went to the laundry. She never, ever, went anywhere else but on this particular morning I needed to see that old Merc parked in front of the Washateria.

It was there, so I gunned back home and began my loading. At this time I was driving a little Ford Ranger with a camper over the bed. Called it a half-breed truck. I had planned to load in an orderly manner but I was so nervous I started flinging everything in the back end.

After about fifteen minutes my old heart was going thunk thunk thunk. I thought I was about to pass out. I had written rules into the Flight Plan and one said Absolutely No Drinking. But I felt the entire plan was about to collapse so I got the Evan Williams bourbon out from under the sink and took a big pop, right out of the bottle. After that I was able to get up and go on.

I had no trouble following directions of the Plan but I recorded some strange sensations. When I was carrying the armload of clothes along the hall I felt that I wasn't really doing this, that it was somebody else, a stranger. What's this person doing in my house?

Once I thought I heard a car door slam out in the garage. But the sound was from across the street.

When I was going out the door with my last load, next door neighbor Merle Peniston came walking around the front corner of her house, and into the side yard. Before she saw me I ducked back in. Couldn't afford a conversation with Merle. It might take forever. For five of the longest minutes of my life I stood in the house, entreating Merle to disappear. "Go back in your house! Hurry! Go! Go!"

At last she went, and I pitched the final load in the pickup and checked the Plan, which showed two items remaining.

One was the note I'd written in advance, telling H. I was gone, that I'd become so unhappy I simply couldn't stay any longer and I needed to split. I included a raft of details, explaining why I was leaving. I know, these were the things I should have had the guts to say to her face but I wasn't able to do that. It was all I could do even to write them.

That note I taped on the refrigerator door, and went outside and said goodbye to Cher, Becky's Shetland sheep dog we were keeping. That pup was a sweetheart. I have wondered if any of the neighbors saw me sitting on the back steps, hugging a dog.

I drove to the bank, because I had less than five bucks on me. In those times it was customary to check the balance before drawing any significant amount. I don't remember what the balance was but I took out 50 bucks, stopped at Lampo's Gro and bought a six-pack of Pearl, and headed down Highway 6.

I now have absolutely zero recollection of driving from Bryan to Ellen Belle's house in Pasadena.

Several months of unpleasantness followed my departure, while details of a divorce were worked out. All this was hell, just pure torture, and I don't want to deal with the particulars right now.

That was a rough time for me because I had to keep the column going during all the arguments. It wasn't any picnic financially, either, because for almost a year I sent half of every dollar I made to H. I did that until we were divorced.

Five years later I was doing the same things—running from a marriage, and getting a divorce. But leaving Pasadena was easy compared to Bryan.

22 MARCH

Around four P.M. on Tuesday March 14 I took a shower here at Winedale. When I was drying off I developed a mild headache, unusual for me. I almost never have headaches. This one was in the front of my head, around my eyes, which took on a sort of heavy feeling. An eyeache, rather than a standard headache.

After I dressed and went in the kitchen, I began slurring words. Didn't think much about that, since I've been having occasional trouble getting certain words pronounced ever since I turned ninety.

Babette called Dr. Hoermann. Got her on her cell phone. Quick as the doctor heard about my speech difficulty she told Babette to give me three baby aspirin to chew up, get me in the car and take me to Methodist Hospital. Right now? Yes, right now.

By that time it was already dark and we're two hours from Methodist Hospital so I figured we'd never do what the doctor ordered. Babette has been trying to avoid driving at night, and that trip to Houston after dark can be wicked.

Also we've got a spoiled dog that can't be left alone for very long up here in the country. In normal circumstances we could take her with us to Houston and leave her in the apartment. But the apartment building is undergoing a complete asbestos removal project and our unit is sealed off. We can't even go in it.

Babette called the vet who does Rosie's med care in Brenham.

Got him at home. It's about eight P.M. now. She talked him into saying he'd send one of his staff members out to meet us at the clinic and take Rosie and put her up while we were in this emergency.

Then Babette packed what we might need at the hospital, and loaded the car. She wouldn't let me lift a thing. Thought I was having a stroke.

By 8:30 we were gone. Weather was good and traffic not too bad. By 11 o'clock we pulled up to the Methodist ER. I was still having symptoms but not often and not severe. We were relieved to see that the ER was not crowded with patients waiting for treatment. I got immediate attention. (Our doctor called, told 'em we were coming, alerted the hospital's stroke team.)

I was having no pain but my BP was 216 over 100-and-something. I was put in a wheelchair and taken for a quick CT-scan on my head. A doc appeared and asked a flock of questions and gave me the stroke test, which I've had many times before during routine exams. How many fingers do you see? Can you feel this? Can you feel that? Does this feel the same as that?

Then into a weird room decorated with dials and shiny equipment where I was undressed and put in a gown and hooked up to a major league EKG rig. I noticed my BP by then was down to 166 on the top number. Couldn't see the bottom number. My speech symptoms had gone away now.

Another doctor appeared, two more nurses and I don't know who else. All talking, mostly to Babette, about me, as if I weren't there or maybe unconscious.

A nurse tells us there'll be more tests to come, but for those we'll need to move to a room up on the stroke floor. Right now, though, no room on that floor is available so we'll have to wait "a while". Then, placing a finger aside of her nose, up the chimney she rose, taking all the doctors and technicians with her, and we never saw them again.

I believe it was at least 3 a.m. before we got out of that room. Poor Babette. She was the one doing the suffering. All these hours, far as I know, she didn't even have a place to sit.

Finally they rolled me up to the sixth floor and put me in a fresh bed. Nurse Novocain came in and asked all the questions I had already answered downstairs. She said I could go to sleep if I wanted to. I wanted to. So I covered up and almost had my eyes closed when a guy in blue coveralls appeared and asked if I were claustrophobic. I said I was not, but the next time anybody asks me that question, no matter what color coveralls they're wearing, I'm saying yes, because a no answer gets you a cute little test called an MRI.

Here's what happens when the MRI is testing for stroke: They lock your head in a harness so that you can't move your neck. They slide your body into the bowels of what feels like a tomb and for forty-five eternal minutes they bombard your head with nasty, thunderous, shattering noises. They quit at forty-five minutes because fifty minutes of that punishment would give the patient a stroke if he had none when he came in.

But that test gave us three results, two favorable and one negative. While I was being bombarded, Babette was allowed to lie down in my bed. That was one of the favorables, even though I don't think she did any sleeping. The other positive was that the test showed I had not suffered a stroke. The negative result was that they served us a breakfast of powdered eggs.

Now comes Dr. Lasek, a trim little physician who works as a hospitalist at Methodist. I start liking her right away, despite that she thinks I'm man-stubborn because I don't drink enough water. She agrees we're doing the right thing by not having surgery on my hernia. She decides from all the tests that I've had a TIA—transient ischemic attack.

A TIA is an almost-stroke, a serious symptom that hints strongly that a full-blown stroke might follow, sometimes within a few days.

Dr. Lasek springs us from the hospital. Babette finds us a place to spend the night, in a guest room at our apartment building. We fall into bed, get up early and drive back to the country, rescue Rosie, and here we are at Winedale without a stroke, so far.

7 APRIL

More than three weeks now since the TIA adventure, and no sign of more stroke symptoms. The first week I tip-toed around the house as if I might fall over dead if I tripped on one of Rosie's toys. The second week I was allowed to walk around outside, long as I didn't lift anything heavier than a tennis ball. The third week I was permitted to drive my pickup, alone, five miles to the Post Office in Round Top. This week I've been encouraged to mow the yard but I haven't done it yet.

I no longer get my one glass of wine per day. I don't get anything alcoholic. Well, a bottle of non-alcoholic beer, which tastes exactly like beer without any alcohol in it. A little better than nothing.

I figure if I can get past another two weeks without a stroke, I might make another year or two.

Meanwhile, life here at Winedale is pretty well what it's been the last few years, with me not doing much other than washing dishes. We do have a plan now, and it does not include any heroic drives to Houston in the middle of the night. When I have symptoms, we'll drive twenty-five miles to the ER at the Brenham hospital and tell 'em to call the stroke team at Methodist and follow directions. Our doctor has set this procedure up and we're OK with it. Feeling pretty good today.

I see that on the 7th day of this month I wrote that I might last another year or two if I didn't have a stroke within the next two weeks. Well, the two weeks have passed now, or almost, so I'm going back to what I've been calling routine activity. Lifting 3-gallon bottles of water, putting out the garbage, driving my pickup to the Post Office and back.

Word of family trouble comes from Houston. Mark has had a wreck, not unexpected. Ran his car off the road during a rainstorm, hit a highway road sign, injured a knee seriously, totaled the car. Lucky he wasn't hurt far worse.

Ambulance hauled him to hospital for emergency treatment, but he had a severed tendon on that knee, and has since had surgery and will live on crutches for weeks. Becky is seeing him through this mess. Feeding him, caring for him. Without her he would be—who knows? She's been doing this for years, and is plenty sick of it. Not much I can do to help. We can't even go in her house because she's got this damn mean little feist dog that attacks anybody who walks in. Last time we were there it bit Babette, twice, on her ankles so she is not enthusiastic about returning.

Nothing very smiley to report lately, except that the Astros are off to a favorable start, knocking homers and leading their division.

Back to unhappy: Month ago we spent almost $4,000 repairing the spillway on our tank here at Winedale. Then here came a three-inch thunderstorm last weekend and just about destroyed the repair job. Guys who did the work just left here after eyeing the damage and talking about ways to fix it. We'll see.

22 APRIL

It's love bug time. They're everywhere, everywhere, flitting around in tandem or flying solo in search of partners. Down on the coast, in that marshy country, some years these strange insects can get so thick they'll clog automobile radiators and cause engines to overheat. Remember what we used to call 'em? Telephone bugs—say hello and hang up.

Back in my high school days, boys enjoyed love bug time because there it was, sex, filling the very air, and they could make bad jokes about it and get the girls, as they imagined, thinking about it. If the girls were as interested in sex as the boys were, we'd have seen uncontrolled screwing going on in the halls at school.

BP 168/80—Too high. It's the result of eating a bait of Mexican food, which is loaded with salt. My pulse, at rest, remains slow, in the low 50s, and that's good. The risk of stroke, they tell me, is greatest when both my pulse rate and BP are high. I take a dose of Bystolic to keep a low pulse rate. Pills, pills.

4 MAY

No journaling lately because Babette and I both have been sick. Two weeks for me, and now she's in the middle of her own version of the same bug. This feels like the flu to me, even though we both had flu shots. Pretty miserable, for both of us.

But far worse for her. She has a chronic cough and this flu-cough, or whatever it is, creates a huge aggravation. What aggravates the aggravation is that we have tickets to fly to New York so Babette can see her grandkids early in June and this sickness is threatening that trip. We're hearing on the Internet about "uncommon colds" going around and lasting for weeks.

This will be a catchup entry. Lots been going on lately, some of it good but most of it not. Babette's having tough time getting well, that's been the worst of it. She hasn't been out of this old house in almost three weeks. Little better last couple of days.

She's now eating what I cook, sometimes. That tells you how rotten she's been feeling, unable to stand in the kitchen and fix her own meals.

We've come to agree on this: Living in the country has its rewards, but it's a damned poor place to be sick. Drugstores and doctors too far away. If we'd been in Houston I'd have had Babette in the hospital.

Good news? OK, how about them Astros? They go up to Yankee Stadium and whip the Yankees three out of four games.

And then I had a call from Philip Spitzer, my literary agent I haven't heard from in 10 years. Phil said get in touch with Dick Atkins (of Atkins Films, Inc.) because there's renewed interest in a film based on my *Addison* novel. Atkins has held an option on that book for maybe twenty-five years, although he does seem seriously forgetful about renewing his claim now and then with a check.

Still, hearing the term "renewed interest" in a movie deal increased my old pulse a few beats, so I had a long talk with Atkins. Turns out the renewed interest came from Dick himself. He'd just celebrated his sixty-sixth birthday and had whomped up a fantasy in which he had produced a movie based on my novel and it was making enough money to build Trump's Fence on the Border.

This doesn't mean a thing. It is just Dick Atkins being Dick

Atkins. It's his way of saying he'll keep trying to raise millions to make my film, provided he doesn't have to send me anymore money to maintain his option.

17 MAY

Family news. Kacy Hale, my granddaughter, is moving to Houston. On next July fifteenth she goes to work as a registered nurse at a new med center down in the Clear Lake area, where Becky and Mark live.

This could be a positive development, for Becky and for Mark. Kacy talks a lot about her father being her favorite person on earth and how much she cares about him.

21 JUNE

We're home (Winedale, that is) from ten days in New York and that trip was super-hard on both of us. I shouldn't have gone but we couldn't figure out any way to leave me here so I went. Spent a lot of money and my BP spiked, so I mostly stayed in the hotel room and looked out the window.

I used to enjoy going to NY but it's now too much for me. Everything moves too fast and makes too much noise and costs too much. I doubt I'll ever make it back up there again.

But Babette accomplished what she went up there to do. Pitched her novel to five genuine NY agents, and had a good visit with Will and Maren. And the grandkids, who are two beautiful and intelligent children.

BP today 149/65. I don't worry about 149 any longer. My BP is so jumpy it ranges all over the map, reacting to whatever's going on in my life. I can feel it rising and falling.

22 JUNE

I've just now read over the last few entries of this journal and I'm a little surprised by all the negativity. You'd think we were about to move to the poor farm, or the graveyard. When the truth is we ought to be going to church and sending up thanks for our good fortune. We are, for instance, so lucky to have this old house in the country to live in while our apartment building in Houston is being torn apart and rebuilt. Many of our neighbors in that building have in effect been flat forced from their homes.

I think the election of Trump was such a dreadful shock to Babette and me that we tend to think in a negative way about almost everything. I told friend Bill Gould the other day that since the election I feel like I'm watching a bad movie about events going on in a country that can't possibly be mine.

26 JUNE

Measured inch and a half of mostly gentle rain. No high wind or violence of any sort. Slow run-off from the watershed that added several inches to level of the tank. Thanks for that.

Phone call from Becky who says Travis is moving to Texas with Kacy and her husband whose name I can't remember[3]. Apparently Travis intends to live with Kacy and what's his name. They've rented an apartment which I hope has more than one bedroom and—hear this—Travis has found a job down here already. I wonder if anybody else is coming.

Me? Oh, I'm feeling about as well as I ever expect to feel. Had a fair night's sleep last night and that's rare. Spent most of it sitting up, against my sponge rubber wedge and a couple of pillows.

---

3. Brandon is his name.

My mystery discomfort still won't let me sleep very long all stretched out on my back, or even on one side or the other. It's a mystery to all the doctors we've talked to about it. A pain that goes away when I stand up.

We do laugh at times about this curious ailment. But I've got a serious notion that it's not going to end well.

20 JUNE

Yesterday we made a grocery run. Got up early, left Rosie in day-play at Brenham Vet Hospital, drove down to Katy. Loaded up on organic veggies at Whole Foods, had an inorganic lunch at Carraba's, came back home. Now we're enjoying the flavors of true vine-ripened tomatoes. Living in the country, but speeding to the city to get tomatoes that taste like tomatoes grown in the country. How peculiar is that?

2 JULY

A while back I was roaming on the Internet and saw an ad pushing wooden armadillo traps, made by an outfit in Mississippi. Price, $100.

I already have three armadillo traps in the barn. They're made of metal, heavy wire. I've not caught my first dillo with any of these metal traps.

That ad said a wooden trap was better because dillos operate mainly by smell and the wood absorbs what armadillos like to smell and that's other armadillos. And for a hundred bucks I could get a trap that already has that odor.

That made some kind of funky sense to me so I ordered a wooden trap. What the hell. If it didn't work I'd just add it to my collection.

When it came I laughed. It's a heavy box about a foot high and maybe two feet wide, with holes and slots and string and squares of loose plywood meant to move up and down some way or other. Looked like something Rube Goldberg made when he had one too many.

But I wasn't disappointed. I'm accustomed to buying things on the Internet that I can't use. I couldn't use this strange trap because it weighed too much—thirty pounds. I'm not supposed to lift anything heavier than twenty-five pounds.

My plan was, when I ordered the trap, if I caught an armadillo I'd pick him up, trap and all, load him on my pickup and drive him miles away. Turn him loose in a neighborhood that needs armadillos worse than we do.

But since the trap was already five pounds over my lift limit, even without an armadillo in it, I abandoned my plan. Left the trap on the front porch and went to town to get a tarp to cover it up, so visitors couldn't see what I'd bought for a hundred bucks.

While I was gone, Jordan came. Jordan runs an operation he calls Country Butler, out of Fayetteville. He and his workers will come to your place and do things that you can't do, or don't want to.

He came in the back way and met Babette who told him I had bought an armadillo trap that I can't lift and would he pick it up and get it off the front porch. He said he would. While he did it, they discussed the fine points of the construction and concluded that the trap wouldn't work.

During the night I heard a rattle-y, woody racket out in the front yard and the next morning my trap had a fine fat armadillo in it, weighing at least fifteen pounds (my estimate).

So now with its cargo the trap weighed forty-five pounds, considerably past my lift limit.

We have a handy two-wheel dolly and I worried the trap onto that dolly and rolled it about 200 feet outside the yard fence and turned the armadillo loose. He went staggering off into the woods.

Next morning I caught another one, and gave it a ride down toward the tank and turned it loose. Two for two. Not bad for a useless trap.

4 JULY

A quiet Fourth of July. We didn't go into R.T. for the parade and the other festivities. Too blamed hot.

Armadillo Report: Have not caught any further 'dillos. But I haven't noticed any fresh armadillo damage in Babette's flower-beds. Could it be that all those holes, all that upturned soil, was the work of only two animals?

7 JULY

This morning pretty early I rode the golf cart up to the front gate and mailed a letter, country style. Stuck it in our mail box, that is, and raised the red flag.

Some of these station wagon farmers (that's my old term for city folks who buy rural land and build second homes and pretend to be farmers; or ranchers, mainly; I started using the term in the column in the '50s when the back-to-the-land movement was building momentum; lot of these early second homers bought station wagons and painted the name of their "ranch" on the driver-side door, like "Five Oaks Ranch" or "Cow Heaven." I remember a guy driving a new station wagon around Houston with a sign on the door, "Rancho No Tengo," which translates to "I have no ranch." When station wagons went out of style the city farmers started buying pickup trucks, and they still do.)

Anyway, as I was saying, some of these station wagon farmers get confused about using rural mail boxes. They all want such a box because it seems so quaint and rural for the carrier to stop at their gate and leave mail. I recall a new landowner in our neighborhood who thought the carrier raised the red flag as a signal that he had left mail in the box. But the rule is that the flag is a signal to the carrier, that the patron has left mail in the box for the carrier to pick up.

In my early times, all the rural mail carriers that I knew were males. But today a lot of them are women.

8 JULY

OK, I have a tendency to poke fun at station wagon farmers but Babette and I surely fall in that class, and in the years we've had this little place at Winedale we've pulled our share of dumb-ass mistakes.

Funny thing, though, now that I think about it, when I was tearing around the state looking for stories, the station wagon farmers were the ones most likely to help me do my work. And believe me, Mildred, when you do stuff like I was doing, you've got to have help, somebody willing to open doors so you can get your foot in.

Some of those people became close friends, too. I think of Dick and Peggy Edwards who had a small farm not far from here, outside LaGrange. They weren't country folks. They had an insurance agency in Houston and sold it off and bought that farm because they wanted to live in the country.

Over the years I did a ton of stories in this part of the state and Dick and Peggy helped me do many of them. They understood what I was looking for, and were willing to take the trouble to introduce me to the sources I needed. I became friends with them. Ate plenty meals at their table and slept a few nights in their home.

When you're doing five or six interview columns per week, you need friends like that. Because you're gonna have Monday mornings when you wake up without a clue of an idea how you'll fill your week's space. So you pick up the phone and call Dewey Rickenbrode who runs a little joint (Beer, Bait & Beans) down at Surfside. Dewey answers and you ask if there's anything happening on the beach that you ought to know about and she says, "Come on down. We'll scare up a day's work for you." So by ten o'clock that night you've put in a sixteen-hour day but you've got a full notebook that'll keep you going for another week.

Somewhere in this journal I've written already about Merck Smith, who certainly wasn't a station wagon farmer but he was for years a valuable helper in my work. Just as Georgia and A.C. Herreth were. I visited often in their great old home on Avenue K in Bay City. I was glad to see them when they came to my 90th birthday party at Round Top.

This puts me to thinking about others who ought to be on my list of helpful contacts. In Huntsville, Freddie Smith and Tex Hardy. And Ferol Robinson, head of Journalism at Sam Houston State who gave me a morning teaching job that lasted 10 years and helped pay off our home mortgage.

Nice memory from the 1960s: Freddy and Tex waiting for me to finish my classes at Sam, then we'd pile into Tex's pickup and trail his boat up to Lake Livingston and go fishing, spend the night. Next morning bring back a cooler full of crappie and unload 'em at the back door of the Texan Café where the blue-plate special at noon would offer fried fish with black-eyed peas and cornbread.

Another memory from the work years: It's about five P.M. and I'm driving toward Bryan from doing a day's work down on the coast somewhere. I stop in Bellville and toot my horn in front of the Bellville Times. Franz Zeiske, editor and publisher, comes forth looking serious and important in his white shirt and dark suit.

Without a word other than "Hello," we move on up to the Hilltop Drive-In where the girl on duty hands out two large sturdy plastic cups, each two-thirds full of ice and water.

From there we roll down the other side of the hill and stop in the roadside park on State 36. Franz reaches under the seat for the pint of Evan Williams he knows I have bought at the liquor store by the railroad tracks. He uncorks it and fills the plastic cups to their brims.

I promise you these are serious drinks, sippers. While we sip we loaf along the country roads of Austin County, and we talk. Franz and I were just about as close as friends can get. We were both having trouble at home and we needed those whiskey visits. To talk not just about troubles at home but a thousand other things.

Then at Nacogdoches I had Lucille and Ray Smith. Ray was an oil producer, not one of the rich ones. He dug super-shallow wells there in Nacogdoches County and produced them bucketsful at a time. Yeah, like he was milking cows.

And I had Carolyn Graham at La Porte and all her Houston defense lawyers that she kept up with (and still does but she's gone a long way from La Porte) and Jack Ellison at Buffalo and Buster Curry at Clute and Harold Nichols at Victoria. . . well, there's no profit in making a list. I'd never get them all down and spelled right.

Bill Dannar, excellent carpenter and folk artist who lives a few miles away in Carmine, just wheeled by and left me a nice gift. During Antique Week he sets up a little shop called The Wobbly Walking Stick and sells his primitive art, made of old scrap lumber and dead timber and that kind of stuff.

One day he caught me walking with my cane, so the gift he brought today was one of the wobbly walking sticks he makes and gives to friends. I love it. It's made from a limb of a --------- bush, name of which will return to me presently. Nice and crooked, with my name carved on the side of it.

Crape myrtle. That's the bush Bill uses to make his walking sticks. Most of its branches are knobby and crooked.

10 JULY

Reading over the previous entry sends me back to the day my friend Mel was visiting here at Winedale, looking at my books and the few things I've got on the walls. He said, "Long as you've been in this business, I'm surprised you don't have a ton of loot people have given you. Don't newspaper columnists get valuable gifts from readers?"

I told him that's a myth, far as I know. If I cashed in all the stuff I've been given over sixty-odd years, I doubt I'd have enough to buy a ticket to Kansas City.

Now I've heard that some reporters have taken big money from wealthy individuals that they write about. Maybe so but I don't know any such reporters, and I doubt the truth of those stories.

When I first hired on at the *Post* in 1947, for a while I did a few general assignment pieces, stories that didn't amount to much. For instance, I remember being sent out in Houston Heights to interview an old lady who was in trouble with the City for keeping some ridiculous number of cats, maybe it was fifty-two, or sixty-two. Anyway, when I was leaving she tried to give me a ten-dollar bill. Back at the paper I boasted to Elbert Turner, my editor, that I had been offered a bribe to make that old lady look good in my story but I refused it. Elbert said, "Congratulations." He didn't even ask how much the old lady offered.

A while later I did a story about riding in the cab of a locomotive and the PR guy of the railroad offered me a twenty-dollar bill. I refused that bribe by delivering to the PR guy a sermonette on the high ethical standards of the journalism profession that I remembered from college.

So there you have it—ten bucks from the cat woman and twenty from the railroad guy, for a grand total of thirty dollars in bribes I've been offered over sixty-plus years as a journalist. I've done stories about the homes, farms, ranches and businesses of dozens and dozens of extremely wealthy people but I was never offered a dime by any of those folks.

Sure, there are ways to offer bribes that don't involve cash. Gifts. Favors. I'm told that some newspapers and other publications have a hard rule, that their staff writers must not take gifts, no matter the value, from their sources. I worked for only two newspapers—the *Post* and the *Chronicle*—and I don't recall a gift policy being discussed at either of them. Maybe such a rule was supposed to be understood, a given.

If so I probably violated it.

After a few years on the job I formulated my personal policy about gifts. Here it is working in its simplest form: I'm doing a story on a blind guy who, through amazing resourcefulness, has become a master vegetable gardener. When I'm leaving he offers me a mess of turnip greens worth maybe $1.25. Do I take those greens? Damn right. Because of the spirit in which they were offered. Refusing them would almost be an insult to the giver. And taking them won't make an ounce of difference in the way I write the story.

Even so, my record on source gifts wouldn't do to go in a journalism ethics text. I hired on at the *Post* as farm and ranch editor at a time when a flock of wealthy business and professional Houstonians were getting interested in agriculture. And buying ranches, mostly as a tax dodge.

I met all these guys, and wrote stories about their places, since they were on my beat. One I'm remembering now was a lawyer named States Jacobs. His daddy was William States Jacobs, famous as a preacher and rancher. The Jacobs family had a lot to do with bringing the first Brahman cattle to Texas, and to the U.S.

One day I got a call from States, or probably from his secretary. Message was, go to Stelzig's. So I went, out of curiosity. Stelzig's was famous as a source of handmade boots. When I showed up there a bored worker had me take off one shoe so he could draw an outline of my foot.

Six months later I was the owner of a fine pair of cowboy boots by Stelzig, free of charge. Elmer Summers, who had the same job at the *Chronicle* that I had at the *Post*, told me that Jacobs gave me the boots because I was running around the state, writing about ranches, and wearing my old GI shoes.

It's true that I wore GI clodhoppers. In my work I did a lot of trudging around in plowed ground and tall weeds and brushy real estate and GI shoes worked well for this kind of duty. These were the same pair of shoes I wore on about three quarters of my combat missions.

The Army Air Corps issued, to aerial combat personnel, flimsy electrically-heated shoes (more like felt house slippers) but I didn't like them. Sometimes they didn't work and at altitude the temp could run minus twenty-five degrees and my delicate size-twelve tootsies would freeze.

But the main reason I put on those heavy leather GI shoes, I got to looking down at the Alps. If I ever had to bail out into those frozen mountains, there wasn't much chance of survival. But in case I did get one thin chance to walk out, I wanted something substantial on my feet.

Those hot-shot handmade cowboy boots from Stelzig's? I wore

'em maybe half a dozen times. They hurt my feet. They sat on the floor of my closet for years. I tried to give 'em away but I couldn't find anybody with size-twelve feet, or at least anybody who'd admit it.

21 JULY

We have entered the dog days here at Winedale.

No rain, nor any prospect. Nothing growing, unless it's irrigated with precious well water. White clouds with black bottoms. Temp highs pushing up to 100. Everybody running on a short fuse. Babette and I had an argument this morning, about something not worth the energy it takes to argue.

24 JULY

Up at 5:30, courtesy Rosie, who believes that if a sleeping person rolls over and grunts, that person is ready to rise and dress and do whatever Rosie wants done.

So, on with the early morning activities. Find something to put on. Exercise my legs to get some circulation, enough that they'll let me stand. Take a few experimental steps, checking whether the old knees are ready to function.

On to the kitchen. Make a cup of coffee. Load dishwasher and set it going because I didn't do it after supper last night. Turn Rosie out. Take coffee and cell phone to the front porch, check how Astros came out and see if our president has punched the button to start a nuclear war.

Eat my shredded wheat, with grapes and honey and soy milk. By now it's seven o'clock and Babette is up and in the kitchen for her cup of Earl Grey.

Mornings like this is when I get my hugs. Which is my favorite of all things that I get because she feels so smooth and sexy in her thin nightgown, before she puts on panties and bras and jeans and other unnecessary rigging. These hugs are what we have now instead of sex and I place an extremely high value on them.

Let's see now, where were we?

Oh yeah, I was talking about my morning routine, here in the deeps of summer. If Babette doesn't walk the dog, I perform that duty. This needs from forty-five minutes to an hour. Even though Rosie has an acre of fenced yard to smell around in, she must be walked daily like any city dog. She has her personal route, from the front gate along the road and through the woods to the creek and then downstream to the tank where she bathes in muddy waters. Then back to the house through a heavy thicket in which she hunts for coyotes, coons, copperhead snakes or anything else that might cause satisfactory trouble.

Then I—hold it, we've got a visitor turning in the front gate.

1 AUGUST

Let's start the month of August feeling hopeful. There is reason. The weather people are talking about a front coming down from the northwest, threatening to collide with Gulf moisture and produce a general rain. Up to three inches maybe.

This is supposed to start happening tomorrow, and keep happening the rest of the week, off and on. We could use all three of those inches. Our tank is beginning to look like an unflushed toilet.

At the Round Top Post Office yesterday I met a fellow wearing flip-flops and green shorts with a maroon T-shirt and a great round stomach going along before him. He said he was glad to meet me because he reads my stuff in the paper every day. Said he never misses a day.

I still get that kind of thing once in a while. Ordinarily when people now say they read me every day I don't bother to tell them I retired in 2014 so I've had no column in the paper since then. Because they mean well. They're just trying to be nice, make me feel good. So I thank them for their readership, tell them how much I appreciate them.

But in the case of the guy at the P.O. yesterday. . . I wasn't nice to him. I told him he couldn't be reading me every day because I am retired and haven't been in the paper for three years, and even if I were still working I have never been in the paper every day.

You know what? He wasn't fazed, not an ounce. He said, "Son of a gun." And produced a big hawk in his throat and spat on the sidewalk.

Now I shouldn't have done that. I'm sorry I did it, almost. But since I did, I'm pleased I did it to that dude because I just know he voted for Trump.

3 AUGUST

In the grocery store in Round Top I ran into a fellow from Lake Jackson. He was a friend of Gene Morgan so we talked about Morgan, who was a good man to have for a friend. And a bad one to have for an enemy.

Morgan probably helped me in my work more than anyone. Or maybe I simply enjoyed working with him more.

Thing is, when I went out to the Big Bend Country and hooked up with Morgan, we'd do things that very few people ever got to do. For example: Ray LaBeff would fly his four-seater from Alpine down to Morgan's place on the river, and we'd load up and fly way down into Mexico, land on huge ranches owned by wealthy Mexicans that Morgan knew. And I'd get to see a life style that you wouldn't believe exists so close to us here in Texas.

That three inches of rain they were talking about a couple of days ago? We didn't get as much as a dark cloud out of that forecast.

26 AUGUST

The past few days our attention has been captured by the weather people, who've been talking about a minor tropical depression in the Lower Gulf, down below the Yucatan Peninsula.

We've been patient with these guys because they kept saying they weren't sure where this system would land. Most likely it would creep on in to Mexico and blow itself out over the mountains. But there was a thin possibility that it would walk across the Yucatan, pick up steam from the warm waters of the Gulf, and go inland closer to the mouth of the Rio Grande.

If that happened, the Texas coast would be on the dirty side of the system and it might bring a couple of inches of rain to our thirsty state.

Well, everybody from Ft. Worth to Brownsville is paying attention today, August 26. Because that little Mexican depression last night hit the Texas coast near Corpus Christi as a Category 4 hurricane, and it's just tearing hell out of that touristy region.

And it's already generating hairy adventures far inland, including here in Washington County. We began getting east wind yesterday afternoon and light rain last night that intensified into a torrent before dawn. I have written in this very journal how I love the music of rain on the tin roof of this old house. But this hurricane-bred deluge is not musical. It's hostile.

I was relieved when it eased off about 7:30. I bundled up and rode the golf cart down to check on our tank. It was already full and beginning to run over the spillway. I haven't been back but we've had rain just about all day. It's 4:30 now so I know we have a major action on that spillway. Our nasty little stock tank, full of water at last, and running over.

Now hear this: We're in for several days of this heavy weather.

27 AUGUST

Five P.M. We've been pounded pretty close to constantly with a heavy downpour for the last twenty-four hours. Not much wind, though, so if this is the worst we'll get we ought to be all right.

But Houston is a flooded mess. I mean this is a Disaster. As Buck Schiwetz used to say, it's a catastrophe with a capital K. Houston will not recover from this Harvey storm for years.

Babette and I are feeling so grateful that we have this weird little house in a patch of woods, so far from the flood waters. And yet we're fighting guilt, too, and the peculiar notion that we ought to be in Houston, struggling with the multitude.

Those are our friends down there, losing what they've worked for all their lives. Millie Hast, who sat with us in the hospital through Babette's eye surgery, lost her home and her car. Betty Luman, my copy editor at the *Chronicle*, has three feet of flood water in her home. The same with Alan Bernstein, whom I worked with for twenty years at the paper.

These are just a few we've heard about, while the rain is still coming and the flood waters rising. The storm is giving forecasters an impossible problem. Its eye is trapped between two high pressure areas, so that it can't move on inland and blow itself dead. Instead it's stalled there on the coast, spinning, sucking water out of the Gulf and dumping it on Texas.

I'm nursing an uneducated theory that this thing could sit there for days and days, bringing about a biblical flood. Which is not likely but the international coverage being given this event leads me into outrageous thought.

28 AUGUST

Whew. Looks like we'll survive, without serious damage.

Here at Winedale we've had a day of sunshine, most welcome after the stormy week. Neighbor Henry Ullrich, across the fence to the south, called to ask if we were all right. Then reported that since the storm began he has measured twenty-two inches of rain.

My little gauge holds only five inches. I emptied it twice and it refilled and I didn't go out during the storm to empty it again. So I'm taking Henry's total. We've heard of higher amounts in neighboring Fayette County, southwest of us.

Houston, we know, had a far higher total. More than fifty-five inches. And today they're reporting thirty storm-related deaths and expecting to find more victims as the flood waters recede.

Our little gang of Hale relatives was lucky. Mark and Becky and Kacy and Travis—and Kacy's husband whose name I still can't remember—all live down in the Clear Creek area of Houston and that's lowland, swampy, marshy, flood plain. It's fully developed with residences, business and industry but still subject to flooding and I do wonder how it escaped.

Kacy and her family moved to Houston from Kansas only a month ago. We're tired making jokes about this, how she's already packing up to move back to Kansas.

Houston is a tough city and it'll survive. But it'll take a long time and it'll be costly to all of us who choose to live in this strange place, where no city should ever have been built.

20 SEPTEMBER

Check the date of this entry, the first addition to the journal since a hurricane named Harvey flooded Houston and twenty-five per cent of Texas. And now we have two more storms roaring up through the Caribbean, which is already beaten up by this crazy weather.

On top of all that, Trump has stood before the United Nations General Assembly and threatened to "destroy North Korea." This fool seems determined to start a nuclear war.

In recent weeks Babette and I both have been fighting the symptoms of cabin fever, so we parked Rosie in the kennel in Brenham and loaded up and drove west. To Fredericksburg, to Fort Stockton, to Alpine, to Marfa. At Marfa we rented a little house and stayed a week, just to see what would happen.

Nothing much did. But we liked the cool weather, and Babette seemed to enjoy cooking on the nice gas stove in that little house. The cooking was almost a necessity because Marfa's elevation is pretty steep and it kicks up my blood pressure when I eat in local restaurants. Public fare in that part of the state is almost always too salty for me and my BP.

But this trip we doubled up on my meds and kept my numbers pretty well down into normalcy, and ate Babette's low-salt meals.

We both love that Trans-Pecos Big Bend country. Funny thing, the places in the world that we love best don't like us. Babette, in fact, had more of a blood pressure problem at Marfa than I did, and BP is not usually her problem.

Becky is in Africa, on her once-in-a-lifetime 30-day trip to see the wild animals and all that wonderful country.

She's into the second week now and we're receiving Facebook posts of photos she's taken. Lions and leopards and giraffes and baboons.

I'm pleased she's getting this experience. Beck has taken some swift kicks in her life and she's shown character. She created a career and made herself a useful citizen. Saved her money and bought her home and got up at four o'clock for years and years and made a hard drive to her job and she deserves a happy retirement.

28 SEPTEMBER

I've been trying to decide whether physical exercise at ninety-six makes me feel better, or worse.

Not that I do a lot of exercising. I've started doing light lifting (I do mean light; five pound weights; but I'm so out of shape that those little dumbbells begin to feel heavy after I put them overhead twenty-five or thirty times).

Then I pedal the recumbent bike fifteen to minutes minutes, intending to work on up to half an hour, increasing resistance gradually. At first I thought doing the bike made my legs weaker instead of stronger but I've almost changed my mind now. Seems to me I detect a little more strength, when I rise from a sitting position.

That's the test. Two years ago I could rise from a standard-height seat without using my hands to push. I can no longer do that, at least not comfortably. I can do it, sometimes, by launching my body forward and upward but not without risk of sprawling.

So there's my score on the get-out-of-the-chair test. I'm losing ground. In two years I've gone from can to can't. My goal is to regain enough leg strength to rise, no hands. Until I make that goal, I don't go far from home and sit down without my cane to help me up.

The longer I sit, the harder it becomes to stand. (I used to wonder why motel commodes in rooms for the disabled were so tall. I no longer wonder.) Riding in the car for two hours without a stop has become dangerous, unless I do leg exercises while we roll along the highway. (Pushing feet against the floor board, that is.)

Sitting through a long restaurant dinner can create a problem. Sitting through a banquet-type meal, plus a speech, is a bigger problem. I avoid long gatherings now.

A cane has become my best pal. It has prevented many near falls, serious ones that might have made me a total cripple. Or worse. Fred Hale died from a fall, when he was way younger than I am. Maifred, too. Ima Ruth, carrying all that weight, could have had a fatal fall but she spent her last two years in a wheelchair.

I'd rather die from a fall than live in a wheelchair.

3 OCTOBER

A nice calm half-inch rain today. Countryside looking very little like fall. All that moisture from Harvey has got everything greening up like spring.

Except our birds have left. We're usually working alive with cardinals but now we seldom see one at the feeders. Chickadees and titmice come around now and then. And visiting hummingbirds are still here, drinking my simple syrup.

Don't look now but there's a new tropical disturbance trying to work up a spin, down in the Lower Gulf near Yucatan. The weather people are expecting that thing to become a storm, maybe even a hurricane, and move into the Middle Gulf. But a pretty strong cool front is moving down out of our Northwest, and the hope is it'll bump the storm onto a north heading, toward the Florida Panhandle.

15 OCTOBER

Been lazy the last several days about adding entries. But I've promised myself that I won't be forced to do this journal and so far I've done it the easy way, putting up entries just when the notion strikes.

This computer keeps up with how much I've done. Right now it's showing, down in the left-hand corner of the monitor, that I've written 239 pages, or 51,217 words.

Let's catch up on what's been happening:

That cool front mentioned in the previous entry did deliver

as advertised. It came on down and bumped the hurricane onto a north heading and it went inland on Georgia, or maybe one of the other Old South states. I didn't pay it much attention once it turned away from Texas.

Becky has sent some great photos from her African trip. She says on Facebook today that she'll be heading home in four more days.

Daniel is still working in Houston, settling insurance claims from Hurricane Harvey damage, and Mark is working for him. Good.

The Astros are playing a series against the Yankees for the American League Pennant, and they're one victory away from the World Series. Problem is, they have to win that game in Yankee Stadium. They beat the Yankees twice in Houston—two great games. Scores were 2-1 in both games. If they win tomorrow night in New York, they'll play either the Cubs or the Dodgers in the Series. Probably the Dodgers. Stay tuned.

16 OCTOBER

Becky called to announce that she is home from her long safari. Promised to come to Winedale soon and give us a show of pictures. Said her little dog is mad about being left behind and will not speak to her.

The Astros lost their first game with the Yankees. They will play two more games in New York and must win one to become champions of the American League and go to the World Series.

17 OCTOBER

The Astros also lost their second game. They had better win the third game.

19 OCTOBER

But they didn't. Now they're coming back to Houston where they have to beat the Yankees two straight or they will not be American League champions, or go to the World Series either. The way they've been playing in New York, I doubt they'll win batting practice.

20 OCTOBER

Hey, but they did. Thanks to a heroic 9-inning performance by Justin Verlander, they won Game Six of this seven-game playoff and now if they can take the final game tomorrow they'll be pennant winners and go to the World Series against the LA Dodgers. Trouble is, they've got only one Justin Verlander on the roster.

21 OCTOBER

Nine a.m. This is our wedding anniversary. I'm thinking of Old Friend Morgan. Back in the 1980s when I told him Babette and I were gonna get married, he told me it'd be a mistake to marry a woman twenty-three years younger than I. He said when I get to be eighty years old and sick, she'll still be wanting to go out on Saturday nights, drinking and dancing. Recipe for trouble, he said.

Well, we do intend to go out tonight, to celebrate an anniversary—our thirty-sixth year together.

Ten A.M.—The day is young but I've already had an adventure.

I was walking along the short hall leading from living room to back bedroom. Babette's work station is there, in the bedroom. I started to speak a short sentence to her. I don't remember the sentence. Had maybe six words in it. The first four came forth . . .

but I couldn't get the last two out. I tried the sentence again. Same result.

Babette noticed, of course, as she notices almost everything that threatens trouble. I was showing a symptom of a TIA, a baby stroke. She asked me questions, to make me talk. I could get part of my answers out but couldn't complete a sentence. Or at least not one that made sense.

I've had TIA's before, as you'll recall. They're a serious event because full strokes often follow them, within two weeks. So we're following the TIA routine, which is familiar to us:

Soon as the speech difficulty begins, Babette feeds me a crushed 325-mg aspirin, and encourages me to keep trying to talk. The speech problem, during the attacks I've had, lasts maybe fifteen minutes. There is no pain. Just the strangeness of being unable to say what I want to say.

And that's it. Now, here on October twenty-first of 2017, for a couple of weeks every time I feel the slightest discomfort I'll wonder whether I'm about to have a stroke that'll cripple me, or kill me.

If I had a choice, I'd take the latter.

Ten P.M.—Well, it's been quite a day. About four o'clock I was talking as well as I ever talk, so we cleaned up and went out to dinner the way we'd planned, to observe our anniversary.

Went to this new restaurant in Round Top. Folks running this place have come in here with the notion that they can print a pretty menu and charge New York prices in Fayette County Texas. We'll see. A tourist can already buy a forty-dollar steak at Bud Royer's place on the square. I question whether this country town can support two such places. But then what do I know about the restaurant business?

Babette ordered duck and I ordered rainbow trout. When the

food came I thought my dish didn't look exactly like rainbow trout. But then this woman has coaxed me into restaurants in a dozen different countries where pork looks like beef and fish looks like fowl. So I dug on in.

After a few exploratory bites I noticed a small curly something—looked like a baby shrimp—half hidden on my plate. Showed it to Babette, who identified it as a damn sure shrimp. I am allergic to shrimp.

I didn't intend to eat the thing, so I told B. not to worry. But she inspected the sauce my fish was floating on and asked if I'd eaten any of that sauce. Yes, a few bites. She summoned the waitress and sent her to the kitchen to find out whether the sauce was shrimp based. Waitress came back saying yes, it was, and she grabbed my plate and brought me another. Because—well, well—she had brought me the wrong order in the first place.

We went home not feeling very celebratory, but in time to catch the first pitch of the second game of the World Series. Hell of a game, which the Astros won so now the Series is tied— Houston 1, Los Angeles 1—and Game 3 will be played back in Houston.

I got to bed about 1 a.m., in a little better humor because of the ball game. But still vaguely haunted by the possibility that I'd suffer a stroke before dawn. Or wake up sick from shrimp in the sauce, on a thirty-eight dollar fish I didn't really want.

27 OCTOBER

Hey, look here. Houston has won the third game of the World Series, so we're leading the Dodgers, 2-1. Listen, Houston might even win this thing. We took this Game 3 without using Verlander and without using Kuechel. It never occurred to me that we'd actually win a World Series. This is getting interesting.

Let the record show that at 6:30 a.m. on this date, our feed store thermometer on the front porch of the Winedale farm house was showing thirty-eight degrees.

28 OCTOBER

No stroke yet. No shrimp sickness. But if you're looking for bad news, the Dodgers whipped the Astros 6-2 in Game 4 of the Series. So we're tied up, two games each.

Staying up past midnight to watch baseball ain't as much fun when you lose.

29 OCTOBER

Hoo boy, what a ball game. Game Five of the World Series, with the lead changing half a dozen times and Houston finally winning it 13-12 in the tenth inning.

We're now leading the Dodgers three games to two and the show goes back to California where they'll play Game Six and Game Seven, if necessary. We have a good chance to become world champs and I hope we do it Tuesday night so I can get a little sleep.

31 OCTOBER

It's eleven A.M. on a cool cloudy Winedale day. Rosie the Lab is unhappy at my feet because Babette has disappeared. She's gone out and hired a gang of guys wearing chain saws, and she's down on the creek telling them which trees she wants cut. These are tall dead trees. Babette believes that when a tree dies, it intends to fall at any moment and it might fall on her and her dog as they walk along the creek. So she is frequently cutting down dead trees, or at least threatening to.

Me, I'm confined to quarters with a head cold, sitting here watching the clock, waiting for Game Six of the World Series to start. It refuses to start before seven-fifteen so until then I must dig up something else to think about. I could think about Halloween but I don't like Halloween anymore and I refuse to waste any thought on it.

1 NOVEMBER

The time is now twelve forty-five A.M. on the first day of November and I have just spent five hours watching the LA Dodgers beat the Houston Astros 3-1 in the sixth game of the World Series. I wish I had gone to bed at nine o'clock yesterday.

2 NOVEMBER

Maybe you'll think I'm making this up, even though it's the truth: In Game Seven of the 2017 World Series, Houston scored four quick and easy runs in the first inning and held off the Los Angeles Dodgers to become the world champions of baseball. Let the celebration begin.

10 NOVEMBER

The celebration is still going on, but not here at Winedale. Our recent days have been dreary, because of sickness.

I had a little head cold which Babette caught and that's bad news, always. She doesn't have 'little colds.' Any problem of that sort always threatens to go into serious bronchitis and a truly shuddering cough that hangs on and on. We're into that kind of mess right now.

I'm going to summarize what remains of November because in the last two weeks almost nothing good has happened to people I care about.

The worst thing is that Babette was sick almost the entire month, and she still hasn't recovered totally. When she's sick, nothing in the family works right. Far as I'm concerned personally, when she's sick they could just turn off the switches and stop the world.

Before we leave this November forever, I want to recognize Will Warren for committing what I think was the Bravest Act of the Year. What he did, he loaded a wife and two babies on an airplane in New York City, at Thanksgiving when half the world was traveling, and flew them to Houston to visit grandparents and parents.

Greater love hath no man.

So here we are in December already. Nice cool mornings but we're still sweating through afternoons with temps in the 80s. The weather people are talking about blizzard conditions coming later this week to the Midwest, so maybe we'll get in on the tail end of that action and start feeling a little winter.

I'm looking at the red oak I bought when I was still living at Treetops, before I moved to Babette's house.

I paid twenty-five bucks for that little tree, which stood about 10 feet tall, with a lower trunk diameter of maybe four inches. It was in a three-gallon bucket. I nursed it along on my apartment patio until we bought Winedale. By then it was something like twelve feet tall. Hauled it up here in my old Ford station wagon and planted it in the front yard, too close to the fence and too close to a pair of other trees, both live oaks.

But it has been happy here. Its trunk at chest height is fourteen inches in diameter and its crown must be almost forty feet high.

I'm proud of this tree's success. Because the trees I've planted aren't usually successful. I'm always planting them too close to something, such as fences, or houses, or other trees. This causes them to struggle, and they end up stunted, or twisted, or lopsided.

7 DECEMBER

I'm calling this Mark's birthday, whether it is or not. It's close.

Three days in Mark's life are super-particular in my memory. One is the whatever-day-it-was in December of 1949 when he was born. Maybe the toughest day of my life, because of the long hard labor his mother went through. (I mentioned this earlier.)

I was twenty-eight years old but I didn't really understand what a woman had to endure to give birth, until I stood there all those hours and witnessed it. The experience changed me. I did want a second child and I'm glad we got Becky but I'd have been more comfortable if we could have simply ordered her from Sears & Roebuck.

Then the second day in Mark's life that I'm remembering:

He was 11 years old, and pitched a no-hit Little League play-off game and still got beat 1-0.

(I'm still trying to forget the second verse to that song which came a year later when he was twelve and a better pitcher than when he threw the no-hitter. In our first play-off game, the dude serving as our manager decided to start another kid on the mound, instead of Mark. And the kid got nervous and couldn't find the plate and we got beat. Every kid on our team knew that Mark deserved to start that game. Not one batter on the opposing team had ever faced a left-handed pitcher. Mark might have pitched another no-hitter. Listen to me. You mean to tell me that I'm still pissed off about a Little League baseball game played more than half a century ago? Yes, I am.)

The third day in Mark's history that's still so alive in my memory comes along 10 years later. A brief scene, actually, not an entire day.

He's sitting behind the wheel of that little Ford, on the driveway in the 2100-block of Elmwood Drive in Bryan. Car is loaded with his gear. He's leaving to chase his dream—or is it mine?—to play pro ball in Florida. He's wearing his red St. Louis Cardinals cap and that skinny brindle alley cat is perched on the back of the passenger seat. That cat went everywhere with him.

I don't remember anything we said to each other there on the driveway. We'd never been much good at talking. But when he backed out and pulled away, a painful thought struck me—that he was gone, forever, that the person I had fathered and loved so fiercely would never come back, and I was right.

Of course, I understand now what happened. He simply went away and grew up and became a man. Nothing that came to pass later on has caused me to love him any less. I just wasn't prepared for his sudden and permanent departure.

Then Becky, well, pretty much the same thing, I guess. What happened to Becky is that she grew up when I wasn't looking.

To me, for the first decade of her life, Becky never aged more than 10 months. That's the age I assigned to her and I didn't need her to be any older. At nine months she stood up and walked across the room, and at ten months she was already running—somewhere we have motion pictures to prove this—and she was so small at that age she could run under the dining table without ducking and never touch a curl on her head.

Running. She was always running. I see her gunning down the middle of Elmwood Drive, barefooted, with that old Brownie dog trying to keep up. Brownie, the same dog that went to school with her and followed her around from room to room, so faithfully that when she graduated from his institution, Principal Clyde Bounds issued Brownie a diploma along with Becky's.

Then one day I discovered myself all dressed up, and walking slowly down the aisle of a church, and she was with me, holding onto my arm. She whispered, "Isn't this nice?"

You know what was going on? She was getting married. Married! And I was "giving her away," as they say. What a ridiculous notion. Nobody but me will ever know how close I came to stopping that procession halfway down the aisle, and calling the whole thing off. Because I didn't like that guy she was about to marry, and I still don't, and I'm sorry she ever married him and I'm glad she's not married to him now.

That night at home, her cat padded up and down the hall, giving off the most mournful yowls.

2018

NEW YEAR'S DAY

We're having a little winter here in Washington County. The weather people offered us a forecast of twenty-seven degrees for last night and this did come to pass. So I was a bit relieved to come out of the quilts this morning at six o'clock and find the pump still pumping and the water still running.

One thing we worry about up here in the country is a hard freeze that pops pipes. We know a good plumber but like all good plumbers he gets mighty popular when hard freezes start rupturing pipes.

Babette and I enjoyed the holiday week, just being here together in this old house, cooking and reading and watching a few old movies. All the kids and grandkids are off doing their own holiday things.

We are not sorry to see 2017 go into history. It was not a good year for us. I'm not interested in detailing why. Let's just say we were both sick a lot. Our apartment in Houston was not livable. And we've got that egotistical idiot in the White House, which is enough to screw up an entire century, much less a single year.

2 JANUARY

On this frigid second day of the new year, this old computer is telling me that the journal has reached a total of 65,000 words.

I don't do New Year's resolutions. Instead I do hopes. Here's a short list of hopes that I have for 2018. I hope that Babette's health improves and that she enjoys many more pain-free days of this year. That's my main hope. Then I hope something wonderful happens to her work, that her novel will be published, and her short stories will find a home.

For me, I hope that, one way or another, we can get my nightly-pain problem solved. I'm not asking. Only hoping. I wouldn't have the guts even to hope for anything more. I've already been given so much more than I have any right to expect.

Here's a letter from somebody named Sissy McBride. Says she's a student at Wharton Junior College and her English teacher has given her an assignment—to write to me, and ask questions.

Back when the column was running I got letters from students fairly often. I know they were always assigned tasks. Students aren't interested in my stuff but overworked teachers are always looking for ways to keep kids busy, so they assign them to write to newspaper columnists and TV announcers and county judges and anybody else who might answer.

Sissy McBride asks the same old questions. How long have you been writing the column, and which one is your favorite? So the teacher who gave the assignment doesn't know that I retired in 2014. Never mind. I'm used to that.

It's close to nonsense to write sixty years of columns and then try to pick one and call it your favorite. But when I was working I kept getting the question so I started just naming one that I could remember at the time. Later on maybe I'll walk back through all my clips and try to come up with a true favorite.

16 JANUARY

Hey, it's snowing here at Winedale.

Well, not really snow. Wintery mix, I believe they call it. A few big fluffy flakes, for a while. But mostly what Babette calls invisible snow—frozen mist, which collects in broad patches on the ground and makes good places for elderly citizens to slip down and bust something important. We're staying in.

Temp now is around twenty-seven but we have sixteen forecast for a low tonight. Hoo-wee. I think we've had freezes that severe before, but we weren't here. Pray for the plumbing.

17 JANUARY

The meteorologists hit it on the nose. When Rosie got me out of the quilts this morning at six o'clock, the "thimeter" on the front porch was sitting on sixteen. The house is cold and I'm going back to bed. I ought to turn on a faucet and see if any water flows, but I'm afraid to.

19 JANUARY

We're having the Great Thaw today. Temp up to fifty. Icicles dripping. Patches of that white wintry mix melting, converting to mud puddles.

No sign, so far, of ruptured pipes. Repeat that. No sign, so far, of ruptured pipes. Praise the Lord. The mechanics of this old house took a week of truly hard use, and came through the test bloody but victorious. Let's hear it, loud and clear, for the plumbing and the heating and the plumbers and the heaters.

I'm pleased to be walking around the house today, because I've had another fall, and it could have been the last entry in this journal.

We'd been to Brenham to get flu shots, and groceries, and pills to ease some of our aches, and now we're home, carrying stuff from the car to the kitchen. We're almost finished. Nothing left to carry but a six-pack of beer (non-alcoholic), two half-gallon cartons of soy milk, and a jar of honey.

Babette has gone on ahead of me with a load and she's telling me not to bring everything that's left in one trip. She says it's too much to carry. But I take it all anyway because I don't want to make two more trips from car to kitchen. Wind is cold and my old legs are tired.

I've got the six-pack of beer in my left hand. When I get to the stone steps that lead onto the front porch, I take the first step with my left foot and that left leg collapses and I go down, onto my left side.

One arm partially breaks the fall and my head doesn't hit the ground. My left hip and rib cage land on solid stone. Parts of that side of me pass through a thorny rose bush. One bottle in the six-pack breaks and the first injury visible to me is blood running from the inside of my left wrist. Then I register pain in the left hip and knee joints, but it's not really severe.

Now Babette is standing over me making worrisome noises, and Rosie is there wagging happily. She enjoys my falls. This thought strikes me: Hey, I'm not hurting as much as I should be, considering that I'm lying on a broken beer bottle and losing blood.

Once I managed to worm myself up and onto the front porch, I saw that I wasn't really hurt. The bleeding didn't amount to anything. It was coming from a five-inch scratch on the inside of my wrist. How is that for luck? How many people do you know who can fall on broken glass and walk away with a small scratch?

Well, OK, I did have soreness here and there, including in my old balky left knee, which is trying to shape up and carry on.

But I tell you what, this was my third serious fall, and I'm changing my gears. From now on I'm not going anywhere without a cane, and I'm being careful about carrying stuff. Especially beer bottles.

24 JANUARY

The latest serious development is that old friend Sam Bean has retired. This means another chapter in my life has closed.

When I began going to Houston Diagnostic Clinic for my physical exams—this had to be in the 1960's—Sam was staff dermatologist there. He and his freeze-gun took care of the little crusty precancerous growths that my skin started producing even before I turned 40.

But we seldom talked much about skin. Sam would look me over and shoot the nitrogen to my spots and tell me to come back in three or four months. Then he'd put his doctor gear aside and we'd visit. About baseball (he was raising a high school shortstop the scouts were already following), and about fly fishing, and about WWII. Anything about that conflict drew his interest, and mine as well.

When he left the clinic and started an independent practice I went along with him, and stayed with him, so when he retired I'd been Sam's patient something like 50 years. He used to tell me I have "fertile skin," which I think means I'm always producing warts and wens and moles and keratoses and other dermatological aberrations.

Despite the lingering sting of his freeze-gun, I always left Sam's office feeling entertained, or almost. He sometimes laid on me comical anecdotes that weren't so funny to anybody but him. Here's one that's stayed with me:

He had a favorite bar/listening room where he went weekly for the music. Kind of place where regular customers got casual photos taken of themselves, and thumb-tacked to the walls. Sam had two such pictures there, the most recent taken twenty-five years after the first. And in both pictures, he was wearing the same shirt. "After a quarter of a century, the same shirt!" he'd exclaim, and laugh and laugh.

I have a new skin doctor now. He's OK but I'll miss Sam.

25 JANUARY

What's her name? Sissy McBride. She's the one who asked me to name my favorite column I ever wrote. She's really asking what I think is the best, not the favorite. My personal favorite is the one I did on Babette's and my wedding. But it's not the best or anywhere near. I have no idea what the best is. Might even be one I don't like.

But I wouldn't mind thumbing through the years—mentally, I mean—and remembering a few pieces I think were at least among the best. Many are in the published collections, but not all because some simply didn't fit a book format.

How about this? I'll try to do a few lines about various days of work I don't want to forget, and identify each alphabetically, to set it apart from the regular journal entries:

(a) To start, I like to remember the piece I did on attending a African-American family reunion at Prairie View. I loved that experience, being the only white among more than 200 black people, and feeling so comfortable, and welcome. I stayed all day and was invited to spend the night, and I might have accepted but the deadline made me get back to the paper. I kept a clipping of that column on my bulletin board for years. Likely it was too long to be reprinted in one of the books.

(b) Then the day near Columbus I stood on a country road with a fellow and read out loud to him an entry from The Handbook of Texas. The entry was about the history of his family, and I could tell from his intense interest that he could not read, but wanted to so fiercely. And over the hood of my car he asked, "Where could a man get a hold of a book like that?" If I have ever done any good in my work, maybe that's the day I did it.

(c) The train story. A slow business day in Jewett TX, population about 950. Union Pacific ran (still does?) a fast passenger train through Jewett, but it didn't stop unless it was flagged down by a person of authority. I rounded up about twenty-five kids who had never ridden a train, not even the one that ran through their town. The mayor volunteered to do the flagging down, and we pushed our flock of giggling kids on board. They ranged from six years up to nineteen, and rode all the way to Palestine, maybe thirty miles. With a small motorcade of volunteers speeding alongside to bring the kids back home. Kind of story that made my job, sometimes, a lot of fun.

(d) The moonshiner column. This is probably in one of the collections. I'm proud of it, not because of the subject matter but because of the circumstance under which I got the information. This moonshiner—never mind who or where—agreed to give me all the details on how he cooks whiskey, provided I'd promise not to print his name or his location. Here's a guy who's been caught making whiskey before, so he's got a record. If he's caught again he could be in really serious life-changing trouble. Yet he gives me what I need in my work, taking the risk on the strength of my personal promise.

(e) Hardy Cain was maybe seventy the day I visited him in the woods of Deep East Texas. A maker of violins, by hand. Singer of songs. Teller of stories. For his size he was one of the strongest humans I've met. One fine day he had an idea. He went across the road from his house and built a small rest area, with crude picnic tables. He filled 2-gallon buckets with sand and carried them to a creek branch nearby and dammed up the branch to create a shady pond in the woods. Worked on this project for years. Stocked the pond with fish and left tackle there for people to use when they stopped to rest.

The land where he built his park did not belong to him. He didn't know who owned it, and didn't care. I asked him what he hoped to gain, out of doing all that work. He hoped that some day, somebody would wonder who built that park, and somebody else would answer, "They wuz a old man here, that fixed this place." That's Hardy Cain expressing the fierce desire shared by all persons I ever interviewed: "I was here," they were saying. "I lived, and this is what I did." In Hardy's case, he didn't need to be remembered by name. "A old man" was all he asked.

(f) Cattle drive. Every fall the Huebner Family of Bay City drives several hundred head of cattle from their ranch to Matagorda Island to spend the winter. Right down the middle of State Highway 60 for about twenty-five miles. Maybe the last true Texas cattle drive.

(g) Off-shore drilling rig. Spent a day and night on a wildcat semi-sub offshore rig, to get a taste of the life and times of the people who search for oil below the Gulf. The extraordinary cost. The incredible gamble of such an enterprise.

(h) The Mexico stories. So many of them. If I had to choose one, I'd pick the day I was waiting on the seventh floor of the Hotel Geneva in Mexico City. A situation in which I had great personal interest was going on somewhere in the city, I knew not exactly where. I was obliged to wait for a call so I could not leave my room for very long.

Looking out my hotel window, I saw a young Mexican couple who were living in a hut on top of the building next door. The hut was one floor below me so I could look down into their lives. I gave them names. They had a baby and I watched after it, worried about it when they let it crawl around on top of the building. I was there for ten days, waiting and living the lives of the young Mexicans in the hut. This was one of the strangest experiences of my life.

(i) Europe, where we spent a month while Babette introduced me to France, Italy (of which I saw very little during WWII), Switzerland, Germany. On this trip I sat under a shade tree at Dachau concentration camp and wrote, with a pencil, what Loftis thought was the best day's work I ever did for the Chronk. I don't agree but if I had to pick one of the Europe columns I'd go with Dachau.

(j) The Queen Mary II, one of my personal favorites, probably because I wrote it on board that great ocean liner, on the way to England in 2010. That morning we had sailed over the place where the Titanic went down.

(k) The 30-day trip west with Babette. This would be a series of maybe twenty columns, significant to me mainly because on this trip was where Babette and I got serious. Since then, we've never been apart for very long.

(l) Primavera. Another series, on the annual journey south with Morgan to meet spring. By far the most popular stuff I ever wrote. Not the best. Just the most popular among the customers. A summation of the Primavera columns is in *Home Spun*, one of the collections.

(m) Riding with the prisoner. I was doing a day's work in Texas Prison System, at its Huntsville headquarters, and I met this young inmate who was being discharged after serving a sentence for breaking and entering and possession. He was about to get on a bus to Houston. I'd been talking to Dr. Beto, director of the system. I asked him if I'd be safe in giving that discharged inmate a ride to Houston. Answer was, "Sure, he won't hurt you." So that's how I came to be spending a long day with an ex-con, hearing about his life, at home and in prison, eating with him, shopping with him, driving around Houston so he could show me the drugstores he had broken into to steal drugs. I wrote a long column about that experience. The *Post* ran it in the Sunday supplement and a couple of grafs on the jump got messed up and that, to me, ruined the whole story. I'd like to have that one back.

(n) King Ranch horse. This is a story that Morgan told me. I include it here because it demonstrates pretty well what I call told-stories. That is, somebody tells me a story which is not very good, as told by the teller. But it can be retold, in type, in a style that makes it a splendid story, without changing one fact. Even the teller will like the retold version better than his own. I loved doing told-stories, and did a multitude of 'em.

31 JANUARY

Yesterday I drove the 10 miles from Winedale to Burton to see if I could get the oil changed on my pickup, and get it inspected for purposes of registration. In past years I've been going on into Brenham for this but Burton is closer. and the Internet says I can get an inspection at the Burton gas station on US 290.

So I pulled in there and met the owners Greg Malloy and his wife. I liked Greg's grin and he talked to me the right way. Said he'd be pleased to service my pickup, quick as he finished mounting a tire for this fellow ahead me. Be about fifteen minutes.

I followed him toward the back, because I could tell he wouldn't mind a customer watching him work. He had offered to change my oil but I couldn't see a sign of a lift or a pit, so I got curious about how he'd do it.

He gave me back five of that fifteen-minute wait, slipped into my old truck and checked it through the inspection. Aired my tires and offered a quick lecture on why I ought to be carrying forty pounds in those Michelins. He skidded a big pan underneath the engine to drain my old oil. In a few minutes he slipped a flat-folded cardboard box under there for a cushion, and swung underneath on his back. This was what we used to call a shade-tree oil change, the way we did it ourselves, before we started going to gas stations and garages.

He talked while he worked. Said he'd been in business twenty-five years, there on U.S. 290 in the same place. Born not far away from Burton, headed west when he grew up, huntin' a job and chasin' girls. Travelled all the way to California before he turned around and came back, went to work and got married "and now I've got everything I want all in one place."

Before I drove away he told me to stop in again some time, "see what I'm up to." I believe I will.

Weatherman says it's gonna get cold tonight.

1 FEBRUARY

And the weatherman was right. A tight freeze. Needed an extra quilt on my bed out here on the closed-in front porch. Been sleeping out here lately so my snoring and buckin' and pitchin' won't bother Babette's rest.

Back in December I sent a little year-end note to old friend Campbell Geeslin in New York, and I've been wondering why he didn't respond. I see now why. Here's his mug shot in the house organ of the Authors Guild of America. He died late last year.

Geeslin was a year or two younger than I. We worked together at the *Post* back in the '50s. He was one of our bunch who left Texas and went to New York, to try to make it in the Big Time, and he did all right, too. I have friends who think I should have done the same thing but I disagree. I'd never have survived all that noise and hurry and pressure. I've fought enough of that down here.

21 FEBRUARY

We've taken a month off, to be sick. Both of us had the flu, or if not flu, it pitched a mighty good imitation.

I'm vague on when things happened over the last few weeks but on one of those sick days I had a nice adventure. I lost control of my limbs, and ended up down on the floor and couldn't get up. Scared hell out of Babette. She couldn't get me even to sit up. She called our sturdy neighbor, Henry Ullrich, and he came over with his brother Ray and they hauled me back in bed. I didn't have pain, I just had no strength in my arms and legs. We've since decided that I had become dehydrated, since I always have a hard time drinking as much water as doctors and wives recommend. Anyway, my control returned and I feel about as well as I did before that little dust-up.

I believe Babette thought I was dying. Well, why not? Here's a ninety-six-year-old dude on the floor and he can't move. What else are you gonna think?

22 FEBRUARY

Mail carrier has brought me the annual registration sticker for my pickup, so I'll be driving a legal vehicle until the first day of March 2019. The old girl is fifteen years old and running smooth as milk, I think for two reasons: (Talking about the pickup here, not the mail carrier.)

One, she's never been mistreated. Showing only 80,000 on odometer. And two, I've never pumped anything in her tank but mid-grade gas. Never a gallon of regular.

We're having a decent winter here in Washington County. Lots of nights in the low 40s, and pretty good moisture. I notice a pair of bluebirds already building a nest in the box on the front fence. And our wrens are back, not nesting yet but talking about it. They're roosting on the other half of the porch, near where they had nests and raised babies 20-odd years ago when we first came here. These are descendants of those original wrens, and they return here every year to carry on the tribal tradition. Anyway that's what we enjoy believing.

23 FEBRUARY

I'm just damned if I know what-all is going on with my children. I hear from them now and then but I don't really learn what's happening, or whether it's good or bad.

Now Becky has gone mysterious. She says that she has fallen in love with Africa. No, this Africa is not a country town in Texas. I'm talking about the real Africa, the continent.

The beginning of this little adventure dates back to early 2017 when Becky's bridge playing group, all women, decided they would go to Africa on a safari to see the animals. Which they did with great success, much fun, lots of Facebook photos and messages, as I've reported.

Then back in early December, when I had my experience of dehydration and Babette needed help, she tried to contact Becky. And got no answer for two or three days. Then eventually, these seven words came in:

"I am in Zanzibar with a friend."

Where or what is Zanzibar? When I felt better, I looked it up. It's an island off the east coast of Africa.

Wait a minute. Africa. I got a curious little chill across the back of my neck.

A couple of weeks later, when I could get her on the phone, I found out what the chill was about. She wasn't joking, about Zanzibar. She had really been there, and with a friend. So she had returned to Africa after the safari trip, on her own. She told me, "I fell in love."

Furthermore, she plans to go back again, in April. To see the friend? The one she was with in Zanzibar? I don't question her closely because she's behaving as if she'll give me all those answers when she's ready. I did ask if she was about to get married and she said no, nothing like that.

Becky is sixty-five years old, an independent citizen, and she is entitled to go and do what she pleases, but this business of flying back and forth across the ocean to Africa, as if she's making a quick trip down to Navasota—well, to me, it's bizarre.

19 MARCH

Pretty spring morning. Our live oaks are maybe three-quarters finished shedding, getting ready to pop out tender buds. Then they'll produce those yellow blooms, and shed pollen that tries to cover the world. For two weeks everybody and everything will be shrouded in a sort of sick biliousness.

We have pulled an unintentional dirty trick on our wrens.

We keep an old golf cart in the front yard, for domestic transportation. Saves painful steps from house to barn, and such. When the wrens returned this spring, they looked the cart over and decided to build their nest in it, instead of in the watering can on the front porch where they usually build.

They got the nest about half done, in a compartment on the dashboard. I keep rusty tools that I never use in that compartment and we didn't notice that a bird nest was being built in there. So here came Babette and went driving away in the cart to take Rosie down to the tank for her daily swim.

Enter the wrens, who had been out harvesting straw to finish off their nest. I was sitting on the front porch and I never before heard such a storm of ugly words come out of two little bitty birds. Their nest, gone, plus the entire vehicle that supported it, and they were inspired. They spit out terms of avian profanity that would bring a blush out of a Portuguese sailor.

31 MARCH

My mother's birthday. She'd be 132 years old today.

When I went to Round Top Farm and Ranch for sunflower seed this morning, I saw a woman who looked like her. Or maybe she just reminded me of Mama. The way she stood, when she was looking at something she didn't quite understand. So still, and leaning a bit toward the target until she figured out what it was, or decided it wasn't worth the effort. Then she'd relax the grip on herself, produce a little snort, and go on. I've seen her do that a hundred times.

Leona May Oxford Hale.

Leona? Yeah, that's where I got my name, out of Leona. I've always hated the name. I think Mama hated it as well, because she didn't use it. I never heard her answer to it, not one time. She was May, not Leona, and then when I joined the family they came within one letter of giving the name to me. Oh well, it might have been worse. A new baby is without defense. They could have named me Mildred, or Mary Louise.

Mama was a working person. No, not for money. She worked for family, for people she loved. One time I asked my older sister Maifred if she'd ever seen our mother just sitting around, doing nothing. "Never," she said. "Not one time."

Mama was also a fighter. Her opponent was the Devil.

Early in my growing-up time, she convinced me that the Devil lived in our house, and that he would encourage me to become a greedy, selfish, dishonest boy. When I showed symptoms of acquiring such characteristics Mama would say the Devil had got hold of me. Then she'd kick him out, by reciting selected verses from her Bible. She said these were verses the Devil couldn't stand to hear. I'm pretty sure what Mama enjoyed doing the most was giving hell to the Devil with her Bible verses.

Her favorite verse was John 3-16. It was taught to me as, "For God so loved the world He gave His only begotten son, and whosoever believeth in him shall not perish but have everlasting life."

I must have been about eighteen when Mama acquired a pet bird, a little parakeet. It lived in a cage which stood beside Mama's ironing board. Day after day, while ironing she would recite John 3-16, over and over, until at last she announced to family and friends that she had taught her parakeet to recite that verse.

I will say this. I heard that bird make a lot of noise, and none of it sounded to me anything like a Bible verse. But then who knows what a bird is saying when it opens its beak.

This bird was with us for several years. Sometimes it was turned out of its cage to flit around the house for exercise. One day it found an opening and flew away, and never returned.

Occasionally, when I am letting my mind entertain itself, I think about a certain woman who lived maybe a mile from my family. She is standing at her kitchen sink, and a parakeet lands before her on the window ledge, stretches its neck and tweets:

"For God so loved the world. . . "

16 APRIL

It's ten-fifteen A.M. so I suppose Becky has arrived in Africa. She was due to leave yesterday. Told me a week ago that she'd call before she left but she didn't. There's something about this Africa deal that she doesn't want to talk about.

Hey, somebody in a city-looking sedan just whipped through our front gate. Here in the country we don't get many sedans so I'll go out to meet him.

Sedans can mean missionaries, or lightning-rod salesmen who'll want to come in and stay half the day. They need to be met outside and headed off.

I divide callers into three general types. Start with the Locals. The Locals have been here always. They were born here and they'll die here, often on the land their forepeople settled in the 19th century.

No one can move in and become a Local, even though some do try, and spend years working at it before they see at last that it's not possible.

The second major group I call the Sometimers. These include the people out of Houston and Austin who have bought rural real estate, built second homes on it and are messing around at "living in the country." They are frequently called Weekenders because they join us late on Friday. Then late Sunday they go back to Houston, or wherever their real lives are. We won't see them again for a week.

Some of the Sometimers go in the cow business and keep a few saddle horses. And build permanent homes, even though they're several years short of retirement. Idea is that when they do retire they'll unload their city home and come live what's left of their time here in the wilderness. (Which is beginning to get a bit crowded already.) But they'll still be Sometimers.

Better remind you that this is my personal system of classifying the people who come through our gate. Its weakness is that it's being done by a Sometimer.

Babette and I are Sometimers because we bought land (a little) here at Winedale years before I retired, and Babette isn't retired, yet, not fully. (I doubt she'll ever quit.) We've been paying taxes on this place and living here off and on for more than twenty-five years. So we're Sometimers, purebred and registered, and that's what we'll remain, long as we last.

The third and final class I call Tourists. This includes everybody else. Tourists are legion.

They're the citizens out of Houston or Austin or wherever who are looking for bluebonnets. Or for the B&B they rented on the Internet. Or for U.S. 290, because they've been wandering on country roads and gotten lost and need to get started toward home. We've had Tourists come in and sit on our front porch when we're not here. Or fish in our stock tank and leave litter behind.

Most of our incoming traffic consists of pickups, which are generally harmless. Then we get various shapes of vans, which mean deliveries. Tractor now and then. That's about it.

Driver of the sedan today is a tall slender fellow with a good strong handshake and a name that needed spelling. Amrhine. Don Amrhine. When strangers approach this old house, before they introduce themselves I try to guess why they have come. First clue, he's wearing short pants, so he's not a Local.

He's not smiling so this is no friendly get-acquainted call. In fact, his face is showing moderate trouble. Or I may be misreading that expression. Maybe I'm seeing hurry, rather than trouble. Let's hear what he has to say.

"I've lost a steer."

What that means is that this animal has gone through a pasture fence and is on the loose, probably roaming on property that doesn't belong to his owner. In a few more quick words, Amrhine explains that the animal is not an ordinary steer. He's a Longhorn, with a 4-foot spread of horns and has just recently been brought into this area. So he hasn't had time to settle down and he won't be easy to handle.

Little wonder that Amrhine's face is showing trouble, because he's got problems—finding a runaway Longhorn that's in a bad humor, and then getting it back home.

I told him we'd watch for his steer, which would be pretty easy since we've got only 10 acres of pasture. A steer with a 4-foot wrack couldn't hide very long on 10 acres. But I took a mobile number, just in case, and Amrhine gunned on down the road.

We've had visitors like that before, looking for strayed animals. Not Longhorns, though. Usually calves, which can find a way to crawl through any fence and go trotting off down the road to get in trouble.

Once we had a nice 2-year old Brahma-cross heifer walk through our gate. She liked being here, and stayed a week before her owner even knew she was missing.

Then we had a jenny that tried to take up with us. A jenny is a donkey of the female persuasion. I thought she had an attitude. Her owner was a widow woman living two miles north. She explained the reason for the jenny's behavior: She was in heat and when she was possessed by that condition she often climbed fences and roamed in search of relief.

We've had people looking for lost dogs, and dogs looking for lost people. Once we had a dog accompanied by a Spanish goat. The two were inseparable. They went gate-to-gate in our area for at least ten days, apparently hoping to find a place that looked like home. A week after they'd tried us, a rancher (he's a Local) whose place is in neighboring Fayette County stopped me on the road and asked, "Are you missing a dog and a goat?"

Better catch up, since I haven't made an entry for several weeks.

We've travelled a little in the last month. Babette was getting nervous about the way the world is running under the influence of our idiot president. When her nervousness, or whatever it ought to be called, reaches a peak she has to go somewhere. Europe, preferably, but almost anywhere outside Washington County is better for her than staying put.

I used to have trouble staying put but I kept on the go so long that I finally got over it. I don't much care where I am now, as long as my girl is with me and there's plenty to eat and a way to keep out of the weather. My girl is the main thing.

Instead of Europe we went to Galveston. Checked in the Galvez Hotel, to watch the surf and the pelicans. Stayed four days and nights and the pelicans were wonderful. Pelicans are good for us.

We always have two or three minor adventures when we visit Galveston. The second afternoon of this stay, a certain elevator in the lobby of the Galvez stopped working. It happened that this was the only elevator that would take us to our room, which was on the eighth floor. Don't ask me why. The Galvez is old, and full of strange circumstances.

While we waited in the lobby for the elevator to behave, the manager of the hotel appeared. He asked if there was anything he could do for us, other than fix the elevator. He explained that his hotel was partially occupied by ghosts, who were probably responsible for the lame elevator. His name is Stephen Cunningham. Babette thought he had a good face. She studies faces.

Mr. Cunningham said we might be waiting a long time, so how about if he put us in a room on the 5th floor where we could wait in private. But we refused because all the pelicans were soaring at the 8th-floor elevation and there is no reason for us to be in Galveston if we can't stay at the same altitude as the pelicans.

This is when the elevator fixed itself. But Babette didn't want to get on it right away. She is suspicious of all elevators whether they're working right or not. So Mr. Cunningham rode up with us, all the way to the 8th floor, to be sure the thing was behaving. I suppose this is the sort of stuff they teach you to do, when you're studying to become the manager of a hotel.

Next morning we went down to breakfast in the huge dining room in the Galvez lobby. The menu mentioned a Belgian waffle with maple syrup. Babette ordered that along with a side of sausage. She took one bite and motioned for the waitress and asked her:

"Do you serve maple syrup with your waffles?"

"Yes ma'am, we do."

"Well, this isn't maple syrup that you've served me."

"Oh, yes, ma'am, it is."

"Would you please ask in the kitchen what kind of syrup this is?"

Waitress shrugs, goes to kitchen, returns blushing and apologizing. Guess what. Syrup is not maple. It's some other kind.

"Thank you," says Babette.

That evening, before we went up, we returned to the restaurant to have dessert. We both ordered a dish of Blue Bell Homemade Vanilla ice cream. I should say here that we eat that particular ice cream almost every night at home.

Babette took one bite and told the waitress, "The menu says you serve Blue Bell ice cream."

"Yes ma'am, we certainly do."

"This doesn't taste like Blue Bell. Are you sure it's Blue Bell?"

"Yes ma'am, it's Blue Bell."

"Would you mind checking in the kitchen, to see?"

Off went the waitress. Back in five minutes with an apology. Ice cream was some brand we'd never heard of. It wasn't bad but it wasn't Blue Bell.

Well, maple and vanilla are distinctive flavors, and maybe not
so difficult to identify. I include those two little incidents simply
because I want it recorded that Babette Hale has an extraordinary
set of senses. Especially taste and smell. Most especially smell. If
she is ever sitting in your living room and happens to say, "I smell
a skunk," you better stop what you're doing and start looking for
a skunk.

30 MAY

My birthday, Number ninety-seven. I like that number. It looks
cool. I thought ninety-three, ninety-four, ninety-five and especially ninety-six seemed sort of common. I didn't want to die at
ninety-six so I'm pleased to have that number retired.

During the past year when I told people my age they'd generally smile, and nod. But today when they hear ninety-seven they
say, "Oh, wow!" Just as if ninety-seven is ten years better than
ninety-six.

9 JUNE

Here's the kind of stuff that goes on in your life when you get to
be old as I am:

Back up a little. A few days before my last birthday, I went for
an appointment with one Dr. Laborde, a dermatologist from New
Orleans who has found a home in Houston. I had a mole on my
face that looked suspicious and I wanted this skin doctor to pass
judgment on it.

He said he wouldn't worry about the mole but he took it off and
saved a sample of it to be examined by pathologists, make sure it
wasn't a baby cancer.

He also showed an interest in a little red spot in the shell of my left ear, a place that had been itching now and then and I'd scratched at it. Other than that I hadn't paid it any attention. But Laborde kept returning to the ear in his exam, and he finally decided to do a biopsy on it. Said if it amounted to anything we'd get a report in a few days. So we said goodbye to the skin doctor, went to the grocery store, loaded up on grub and came back to Winedale.

Four days later we got a phone call from Laborde's office: The biopsy on my little red spot? It showed a squamous cell skin cancer, and the need to decide on a course of treatment.

Well, damn.

Cancer, again. First we get colon cancer, and then bladder cancer, and now a skin cancer in an ear. An ear! I've got acres of hide available for malignancy and it's got to pick an ear. I started seeing myself dead and buried and people asking "What killed him?" and Babette answering "A little red spot on his left ear."

But we dug for information and learned that this ear needed treatment, now, or it would metastasize. A scary word, metastasize.

We talked to Karen—Karen Hoermann, that is, our internist—and she recommended a surgical procedure that answers to the letters HOSM, or maybe it's SHMO, or even MOHS. Whatever, it's a procedure in wide use now in the treatment of skin cancer. The way it would work, in my case, the surgeon removes a thin circular layer of skin, under local anesthesia, from the area around my little red spot. Then, while the patient reads a magazine or watches Fox TV, this skin is examined under a microscope to see if malignancy has spread that far. If it has, the surgeon returns to the patient and cuts a little wider circle of skin, to be analyzed. This procedure continues until the doctor finds a layer of skin that's cancer free. Idea, apparently, is to remove all the cancerous skin, while avoiding the removal of healthy tissue. Cancer Surgery While You Wait.

The operation is said by many patients to be pain free, or close to it. What appeals to me is that it can get rid of a skin cancer in one day, a single visit to the doctor. As opposed to a possible lengthy bout with chemo.

We reported to Methodist Hospital for this surgery on June 4. The "we" included Babette and Our Girl Friday, Maureen Huddleston, who is an RN and worked formerly in the office of Dr. Leonard Goldberg, the surgeon who'll do my procedure. Maureen has come along as moral support.

Dr. Goldberg is maybe 70, and a jolly old elf. While he cuts he likes to visit, with anybody who walks in, about almost anything other than the surgery in progress. But it doesn't take me long to see I'm gonna like this guy. He can stick a local anesthetic needle into my ear and I don't even feel it. I consider that a high talent.

He needs maybe fifteen minutes to take a thin layer of skin from around my little red spot. Call this Round One. We'll have about forty minutes to wait, while that sample is analyzed. We go in a pleasant waiting room, where Fox is sharing its propaganda with the world. We turn it off. Maureen brings out some of her moral support—a delicious deli lunch.

While feasting we talk about Houston traffic and what the dog did last night and how we can't remember names the way we used to. But what I'm thinking, hoping, is maybe Round One got all the cancer in my ear and we can rejoice and go home.

Not gonna happen. In half an hour a smiling nurse brings us the news that we must go back for Round Two. And I may as well go ahead and tell you that we had to do Round Three as well. And by this time things were getting a little tedious.

We started this party at 10 a.m. and at 4:30 we're into Round

Four and I'm wondering if I'll walk out with half an ear, or an ear with a big hole in it, or no ear at all.

Before we get the result of Round Four I hear the doctor mention a skin graft. First I've heard of that.

(To be continued.)

29 JUNE

We've been a little busy since I said the ear story would be continued. I'll try to fill you in.

Malignancy in the ear was much more wide spread than I imagined. It covered most of the inside of the ear, so Dr.Goldberg peeled the cancer out and put in a skin graft. The graft skin came from my scalp, a square inch or more. They call this a donor site.

The graft seems to be doing all right. Hair is growing back on the donor site just as the jolly old elf promised.

I've been walking around with a weird bandage on my ear. Looks like I've got a snowball growing out the side of my head. Babette, may God somehow reward her, has become expert at dressing this awkward wound.

Right now the prospect is that I'll escape with a whole ear, instead of a partial one.

10 NOVEMBER

As you can see from the entry dates, I've recently been doing mighty little on the journal. Two reasons.

One, the mid-term elections. It was almost as if our normal lives had been put aside and we were living and working and, yes, praying for a miracle. Which would come in the form of a Great Blue Wave. Americans of all kinds would come to their senses and vote Democratic top to bottom in a Trump referendum and this would take Congress away from the Republicans and place some kind of control on this fool before he leads the country on into total ruin.

The Great Blue Wave did not happen, but a Pretty-Good-Sized Blue Ripple did, and the Democrats have taken the House, and a lot of elective offices across the country changed from Republican to Democrat. So maybe we ought to be sleeping a little better.

The other factor that slowed the progress of the journal was a phone call from Stephen Cox, director of the Eastland High School Band. Seems he is gathering material to publish a history of the band. And get this: So far, his research has shown that I am most likely the oldest living former member of that organization.

And he has asked me to write a chapter of the history based on my memory of being a member of the band. Well. I'm not looking for work but I couldn't say no to that job. Because the friends I made in that little band remained friends as long as they lived, and they were my friends when I was going through the happiest period of my growing-up time, when we were making music together.

Doing that chapter has been tough. Lonesome work, because the only source I have to draw from is my personal memory.

I wonder how many times I have almost reached for the phone to call Ima Ruthie, and ask her to remember a name or a fact. She knew everybody and everything worth knowing about Eastland. I miss her now more than I did just after she died.

2019-2020

NEW YEAR'S DAY, 2019

Hear the noise of the big celebration?

No, because there ain't none going on, not here in the old farm house at Winedale. We did at least recognize New Year's Eve by drinking a bottle (one each) of non-alcoholic beer, and staying up until after 10 o'clock.

Today we'll talk to the kids on the phone, eat turkey-breast sandwiches for lunch, and read the books we gave each other for Christmas. Wow. Maybe I better take couple of aspirin, control the hangover from this wild party.

While I was working on that Eastland Band stuff, we had another health adventure, and this one in many ways was the worst of the lot.

We went back to Dr. Laborde, the dermatologist, the guy who found the skin cancer in my ear. Babette had a suspicious red area on her nose. It's been worrying her so we got Laborde to examine it and he ended up taking a sample for a biopsy.

So here we go again, waiting, to see whether Babette has a cancer in her nose.

And damned if the test didn't come back positive.

17 FEBRUARY, 2020

Well. As you can see from this dateline, the problem with Babette's nose almost put an end to this journal. For an extended period we were faced with the possibility that she would need major surgery on her face that would leave serious scars.

Some cases, similar to hers, require a flap of skin removed from the forehead and grafted onto the nose, leaving nasty scars over a wide area of the face. Imagine how welcome that possibility was. I think I had a harder time with it than Babette did.

All our other concerns, including that fool occupying the White House, were put side while we searched for ways for Babette to handle that surgery, or even to survive the disease.

We ended up returning to our old friend Dr. Goldberg, who operated on my ear. And that rascal came through for us, in spades. I sat in the OR and watched him cut deeply into that nose, and remove (we pray) all the malignancy and, in effect, rebuild the nose and today you can't tell she ever had surgery.

She says the nose is not quite the same but to me it's a beautiful nose, as I told Dr. Goldberg, and he agreed, grinning. Babette says it has a tiny scar running down its bridge but I can't see any such thing. Maybe she covers it with makeup.

Enough, for a while, about doctors and ears and noses.

2 MARCH

A pleasant March morning, with rain promised later on. We need it. We've had a string of moist days the first two months of 2020 but our tank is a mudhole. It needs a five-inch rain, instead of these cloudy sprinkles.

Yesterday Babette took an hour out of her schedule to straighten up the mess I've made on this computer. I've learned to admire what computers can do but I'll never be comfortable operating one of the contrary things.

Main recent change here at Winedale is that politics is now on our daily menu—watching Trump destroy the government, and trying to support those who hope to move him out of the White

House in November. Right now our money is on Bloomberg but I'm not betting the farm on him.

Then let's see, at the end of January Babette and I presented a program sponsored by the Round Top Family Library. We were assigned to discuss how two professional writers can stay successfully married almost forty years while working and living under the same roof.

We got it done, sort of. Drew a full house, too, but I suspect the real interest the audience had was how an attractive, educated woman has stayed married that long to a homely newspaper columnist twenty-three years her senior. Nobody asked that question at the meeting, though.

We got our pictures on the front page of the Fayette County Record. This is counted a rare honor.

When the excitement from that event died down, we talked a lot about the Houston Astros getting caught stealing the opposition's pitching signs by beating on a garbage can.

Result of that trespass was that our field manager was fired, and the general manager as well. I am OK with that punishment. We can do without managers, long as they let us keep important people like Altuve and Bregman and Springer and others who can knock a baseball over the fence.

Wild-caught salmon for supper, buried under rice. And poker chips of XXXXXXX squash glistening with secret sauce. At one time I raised a lot of that squash but never liked it and pitched most of it over the back fence. Now that I like it, with that secret sauce, I can't remember its name.

Where I've got all those XXXXXXX's? Read *zucchini*.

What's secret about the sauce? I don't know. You'd have to ask the cook.

Wow. We've had several hot news days since I last posted. Need to catch up but I'm not sure where to begin. We'll treat it like a three-dot column.

So start with our close neighbor, Randon (Randy) Dillingham, who died last week of Alzheimer's. He was the one mentioned earlier here as the neighbor on the north who in recent times married the red-headed schoolteacher and was a fast shot with a .410. He also exploded fireworks at New Year's and made undrinkable wine with the wild grapes that grow around here. A good neighbor and we already miss him. . .

The Dillingham Family had a lot to do with our owning these eleven acres of woods, and living here at Winedale.
Houston attorney Charlie Dillingham and his son George sold us our land, which was a tiny corner off a ranch the family had owned for many years. Babette went through school with Charles Dillingham, another of Charlie's sons. Their mother, Barbara, was a highly visible woman in Houston political and social culture. . .

But what has us talking and worrying and wondering over the last few days is the virus.
COVID-19, a coronavirus, has attacked our planet, creating a pandemic. People are getting sick and many are dying all over the world. This is the big one, folks. It could kill millions.
The Trump Administration is taking heavy criticism for being unprepared to fight this attack. Doctors are telling us to avoid crowds. Stay home. Wash hands frequently.
Schools and colleges are closing. The Houston Livestock Show

and Rodeo, a huge public event, was in the process of opening. It has now closed. Major league baseball has called off spring training. Here in our back yard, the annual spring antique show which attracts vendors and visitors from all over the country, was scheduled to open in a few days. It's been cancelled. The Masters golf tournament—even it will not be played this year.

More, more and lots more to come, on this virus. . .

I sold my eight-horse riding mower to Ernest (don't know his last name) for $200. I bought that machine for $500 and it was good as new when I sold it. This is typical of my trades over the years. Maybe this is why I am not wealthy. . .

Will Kearney is a new name on our list of iPhone contacts. He lives on a ranch down near Columbus. I don't know his age. Maybe 32? If so, in that time he has grown to a height of almost seven feet and has become a skilled carpenter.

Babette hires Will to come with his hammers and saws and he fixes wooden things that have gone bad around here. She likes tall carpenters and plumbers and electricians because after they fix whatever they come to fix, she asks if they will mind changing a light bulb in the hall that her husband can't reach. They never mind.

I knew Will Kearney's grandfather. He was Charley Kearney, a Colorado County cow man. I sat on the porch of his ranch house a time or two and listened to his tales. . .

We had a crew of tree experts come with strange tools and cut all the dead wood out of our live oaks. I've always depended on the wind to knock the dead wood from our trees, but the head expert said his crew would do a better job, with expensive machinery manufactured especially for dead wood removal. Furthermore, he said, his crew would feed all the dead wood through a mighty grinder that would make mulch out of it, free of charge, and this mulch would be worth many dollars.

So, we have a small mountain of mulch, maybe five feet high and twenty feet long. I expect the dead limb expert was right. This mulch is worth many dollars, which we will pay to somebody to come with the right equipment and spread it around where it might benefit our soil. . .

20 MARCH

The word is out, all over the land. Grocery stores are sold out and the shelves are close to bare. People are stocking up as if a great hurricane is coming.

Just talked to son Mark. He told me about driving to a Sam's Club in Southeast Houston, hoping to haul off a load of grub. Sam's sells groceries in big lots, and has about a five-acre parking lot. Mark said he couldn't find an empty stall to park in so he gave up and went back home.

In one of her recent columns in the *Fayette County Record*, Babette mentioned that it would be helpful if more local retailers would do parking-lot delivery, like the big grocery chains have started. Then customers could call in orders and pick 'em up outside, at a window, or an employee could bring out the order. Maybe get a tip. Customer wouldn't need to enter the store and spread the virus. Or get exposed to it.

Apparently, the message reached Round Top, home of Mercantile, our nearest grocery/hardware. Yesterday Babette e-mailed a grocery list to Merc. We drove the five miles to the store and the owner herself carried our order out and put it in the car.

If that little store can stay stocked, it could be a bacon-saver for us during this pandemic.

21 MARCH

Went back to Merc in Round Top for more groceries. Jackie Sacks, the owner, brought our order out again. She said next time just honk when we get to the parking lot.

That remark took me back to the Great Depression Days in Eastland, when I worked in the drugstores which offered curb service. I wonder if there's ever been a time when retailers gave customers more service for less money. Here's the way it worked:

Two young ladies drive up to Corner Drug on the courthouse square, park out front and honk. I'm inside behind the fountain, working soda jerk. I hustle out to the car, to take the order. Both the girls want a small cherry coke, which costs a nickel.

I go back in, make the drinks, put 'em on a tray with soda straws and two glasses of water. Carry tray out, attach it to driver's door, go back in store. When the girls finish their drinks they honk and I go out to retrieve the tray and collect the bill, which is 10 cents. They give me a quarter. I have neglected to bring change so I go back in, ring up a dime on the register and return to the car to deliver fifteen cents change, thank the girls for their business and invite them to come back soon.

A tip? No, I performed curb service deals of this kind many, many times and I don't recall ever getting a tip. I'm not sure I knew what a tip was at this time, in the late 1930's.

22 MARCH

We have locked ourselves in, against COVID-19. It is spreading, spreading over the planet. Italy is covered with it. In the U.S., New York is the hot region.

Will and Maren with their two children have run to Maren's parents in upstate NY. We will try to ride out the pandemic here in this old house, and feel lucky to have it because Houston is no place to be now.

Mark and Becky and Kacy and her husband are OK there but expecting things to get worse. Haven't heard from Daniel directly but we keep up with him through Mark. He lives in Alabama. I need to check in with Ima Ruth's daughter, Sandi. See how all her folks are doing. Babette has relatives in Amarillo and they are fine so far.

The best friend I have still living in this world is also in Amarillo. He is David Horsley, who married us, and will preach at my funeral. I've mentioned him before. He heard the other day that paper goods were hard to find in our area and he went out and bought up a supply of toilet paper and shipped it to us. A good friend.

We expect to be holed up in this old house for weeks, maybe months. We don't let anybody in, not even friends or delivery people. When they come we talk to them outdoors, and keep our distance. Our goal is to keep from getting sick, to love one another and be patient and understanding because we may be facing a difficult test.

26 MARCH

Spring has sprung in this part of the world. Our live oaks are dropping the peculiar yellow stuff they use for blooms. My old pickup looks like somebody has sprayed it with sickly yellow paint.

We have some pretty nice wildflowers on the place, even up on what we call the Slope, between the house and the front gate. Maybe twenty-five years ago we scattered fifty bucks worth of mixed wildflower seed on that Slope and watched, spring after spring, for signs that even one seed had germinated. Nada.

Now here they come, after we'd quit looking for them. I'm gonna say these blossoms are from that fifty bucks I spent so long ago, even though that's not likely.

Spring seems early to us but it's common for Texans to rush spring. We usually have nice winters but we seem eager to get them over with, so we can move on to our miserable summers.

In mid-February a pair of eastern bluebirds visited my nesting box on the yard fence. They came and went, came and went, fooled around about building a nest and around the first of March a pair of chickadees moved in and took over. For a while I was certain the bluebirds and the chickadees were building nests in the same box.

I'm still not sure who won this battle but I see both the blues and the chickadees coming and going so maybe they've made a duplex out of that box. Must be getting crowded in there.

27 MARCH

Ghost of the Green Thumb has got hold of Babette. She hired Will the Carpenter to build five planter boxes in the back yard, and she has planted tomatoes and squash and onions and various other veggies. These are handsome boxes, elevated on stilts at a height appropriate for a city lady turning truck farmer. All that tennis and golf, back when she was hanging out at the country club, has made something the matter with her spine so that it doesn't like for her to bend down. As in pulling weeds, and digging potatoes.

Now that she has her plants elevated, she worries that they will grow so tall she'll be unable to reach whatever they yield. This is a circumstance that doesn't need worrying about just now but Babette is a pro worrier and, to keep in practice, often worries about stuff that can never happen.

A few years ago I spaded up a plot in the same place Babette's boxes are standing. Planted a veg garden in our native soil and it was a howling failure. Squash bugs got my squash. Bean bugs got my beans. Tomato bugs got my tomatoes.

Now here's Babette, who knows less about growing veggies than I do, which is not much, spending money on planter boxes and irrigation and imported soil and you watch, everything she plants will behave and her crops will flourish. Maybe. We'll see.[1]

Hey, it's raining.

30 MARCH

We have now survived two weeks without Nellie the Maid who is on paid vacation. The house misses Nellie desperately.

The first cases of coronavirus have been reported in Brenham, half an hour away from our hideout here at Winedale. No doubt there'll be many more and soon because people in this area keep moving and working and playing as if they are under no threat.

Babette announces that her son Will is sending us a couple of masks and maybe some rubber gloves, which we can't buy here. Will's father-in-law is a dentist. We bet that's where the medical supplies came from. We are grateful for them. Don't wear masks, yet. But likely will later on.

1 APRIL

A beautiful April Fool's Day, but nobody is making jokes.

Daughter Becky is in a holiday mood, though. Talked to her on the phone. She said she's prepared to spend an indefinite time alone in her house. Little dog for company. Mark comes over to help if she needs any heavy lifting.

---

1. They did not—flourish, that is.—Ed.

She spent twenty-five years working in that Galveston hospital and talks regularly to friends who are still there. They (the friends, that is) are apparently not much impressed with the number of virus cases in the immediate Houston area. Three and a half million people and only 300 reported cases.

Sure, that could change quickly and probably will from what we're told.

2 APRIL

The number of virus cases already HAS changed, overnight. Don't know exactly what the number is at this moment but it's a hell of a lot more then 300 and changing by the minute as more testing is done in Harris County.

Some sources are forecasting that Houston will be the next hot spot. I can accept that, since there's a great resistance among many Houstonians to staying indoors, and keeping separated. For instance, the city has not only closed all its parks, it has taken down the public basketball goals to stop pickup games that draw crowds. People who ought to be staying home.

Babette has about half-decided that we both had a mild case of this virus back in January, before anybody suspected it was among us. We had "light colds," including fever and coughs, followed in her case by heavy congestion and weeks of bone-deep fatigue.

If she's right we could be immune but there's no way to tell without being tested for antibodies and I don't think there's any such test available to us right now.

4 APRIL

I have just finished reading a long piece about pain, in the January *National Geographic*. Scientists all over the world are researching the nature of pain, what causes it, how better to control it.

This gets my attention because of what I call the chronic night pain I endure in my groin. I think it's a complication from the inguinal hernia that should have been fixed surgically long ago. Or maybe it is connected to the hemicolectomy I had in my eighties. Whatever the cause is, I have not enjoyed a decent night's sleep in years.

This National Geo piece touches briefly on a condition in which a recurring pain becomes a disease itself, long after the disappearance of the disease that generated the pain in the first place.

Let the record show that I suspect my night pain has become such a disease.

To sing a happier song, it's raining on Winedale, not enough to strangle any frogs but nicely and gently and perfect for Babette's freshly planted veggie garden.

Last night for supper (OK, dinner, if you insist) she fixed bean soup and yellow cornbread. On a scale of 10 I gave it 11.

Had a long, excellent letter from friend Horsley, who is always doing interesting stuff. He'll be renovating an old house, and in its walls he'll find a primitive tool and nobody will know what it's for. Or he'll suddenly get curious about honeybees, and next thing you know he's a beekeeper with four hives in his back yard.

When he and Michele moved from Houston to Amarillo I thought my God, Amarillo? They'll die of boredom up there, or freeze in January. No such thing. They've both done well there. I don't know, maybe they'd do well anywhere.

I was just trying to think of a male friend I still have, other than Horsley. I cannot. Or a female one, either. I used to think I was good about making and keeping friends. But now, looking back, maybe not.

I worked thirty-two years at *The Houston Post* (at least I was on the payroll that long) and the only lasting friend I made was John Moore, who sat beside me in the newsroom for five years. Campbell Geeslin and I were pretty close for a while but then he moved to NY and I to Bryan and I saw him maybe three times after that. Then I considered George Fuermann a friend. Not really close but then who has ever been very close to George.

Wait, how about Bill Bedell? Yeah, but he was more than a friend. He was my editor, and had a far greater effect on my life than anybody else at the *Post*.

The only real woman friend I made there was Liz Bennett. IS Liz, I should say, since she's alive and probably playing tennis this morning. When I was living again in Houston after my divorce, the gossips had Liz and me in a romance.

Not true, but the basis of the story was that I rented Liz's apartment while she was off on that extended trip I mentioned before. She came back earlier than planned and I slept and worked for maybe a month in the back room of that apartment while Liz was occupying the front. That was enough for the gossipers to put us in bed.

The fact is, at that time Liz didn't need any more romance than she already had. She was hooked up steady with a man friend. As I recall, he went along with her on that extended trip.

No, to me Liz is simply one of the gang, a faithful friend who loved to be helpful, and she helped me when I was clawing through a painful storm in my personal life.

Helen and I lived in Bryan and raised the kids there and the only lasting friends I made during that quarter century were close neighbors. Sam and Myrtle Martin, Merle and Jay Peniston, Brady and Fay Maner, Bob and Mary Frances Robert. Mabel and Steve Pearce. Cheesey and Bobbye Cook.

I get a flush of pleasure out of typing their names and remembering those friends.

Trying to drink more water, see if it might wash away some of the night pain I'm having. That's what the doctors say. Drink more water, more water, more water.

Came awake this morning thinking about my Hale cousins. (Grandma Hale's grandkids, that is). People like Garth Campbell and his baby sister Tommie Ann, whom I have not seen since Maifred's funeral. Also Thomas Minnick and his sisters Lee and Tince. Also Howell Boggus and sister Milabeth.

These cousins were once daily in my life, when we were living on Grandma's farm during the Depression. Garth and Thomas were especially close boyhood friends, back when we were learning things our parents didn't want us to know yet. And I didn't even know whether they were still living.

So, got out my battered old address book and looked up Tommie Ann. She is the youngest of the cousins mentioned above. Last time I heard anything about Tommie she and her husband Johnny Monden were in Dalhart where they owned a drugstore.

After half a dozen rings, she picked up in Amarillo, where she is living now. A widow, age eighty-nine and doing well. She's a regular commenter on Facebook, as I would have known if I'd turn on this computer more often.

She laughs and talks on the phone like her mama did, on Grandma Hale's farm back in the 1930s. (Her mama was Aunt Ruth Campbell, one of my favorite humans that ever walked on this planet.) She told me that those cousins—Lee, Tince, Howell, Thomas, Garth, Milabeth—are all dead. She also volunteered that she and I are on opposite sides politically but that doesn't mean we can't love one another. I took that statement to mean that she is a right-wing pro-Trump Republican.

I gave her our mailing address, in case she wants to send me, along with her love, a dose of propaganda from Fox News.

30 APRIL

This morning about 10 o'clock I heard Babette squealing in the back yard. Looked out there and she was jumping up and down in her vegetable garden, waving her arms. I thought maybe she'd got a wasp sting. She doesn't like wasps.

No, what it was, she was celebrating. One of her plants has produced a small tomato, about the size of a golf ball. This is the first edible object to appear in her entire garden so it's a big deal indeed.

I am glad she didn't plant watermelons. If she produced one of those we might have to hire a band and throw a dance.

2 MAY

This morning the Gladys City Company held its annual stockholders meeting in the back bedroom of our old Winedale farm house.

Gladys City is the name of the oil company that has made a nice living for Babette's family for many years. Babette is its president, so she presides at the annual meeting, taking place this year in our house. All the shareholders are present only via Zoom, which is another of those computer miracles you hear about. It somehow allows the faces of persons to appear on a computer screen here at Winedale even though the persons are in California or some such foreign country. That's all I know about Zoom and that much is probably wrong.

3 MAY

Friends, neighbors and kinfolks we hear from are all asking one another how they're getting along during this weird time, staying indoors and wearing masks and trying to keep six feet away from anybody else.

Babette and I seem to be doing all right, and we have been cooped up in this place more than two months. We were pretty well cooped up here in the same place, by choice, for several months before the bugs came. So our lives are not a lot different now.

Babette is a natural-born germaphobe anyway. In the apartment in Houston she used to piss plumbers off by asking them to wash their hands before touching anything in her kitchen.

Wash my hands? Listen, I have washed my hands so often, when they aren't wet they feel dirty.

21 MAY

Tuesday mornings about 10 o'clock I go to the front gate of our place here at Winedale, to put out the garbage. Sometimes Mark Fiedler, who lives a mile north of us, comes jogging along in his bright orange pants and stops to visit.

The theme of our talks at the front gate is that we are living in an historic time, because of the coronavirus. We stand out there on the country road and speak of deep subjects, with my giant green dumpster between us for purposes of social separation.

Most weeks this is my only contact with a person from the outside world, so Mark's jogging is healthful for us both. Long may he jog.

I remember interviewing a gent who was about to observe his 100th birthday. Don't recall his name. I was probably around sixty-five or seventy at the time.

He talked about falling. He was still getting around pretty well, using a walker, but he had taken a tumble or two and he wanted to talk about it. About falling. How to fall. Good and bad places to fall.

At that time I wasn't interested in falling but now I am.

When I was sixty-five I didn't dream about lasting this long. Figured I'd do good to make seventy, but suddenly here I am old as mountains and falling down is one of my favorite subjects, just like that old guy I talked to long ago.

I get from here to there with a cane. I own a walker but haven't started using it yet. I know I should, but outdoors it takes up too much space and makes people shy away and give me room. I don't like taking up public space.

Falling down is not always a serious happening. Of the falls I've had, only three amounted to much. One of those I wrote about earlier in this journal.

Now I do practice falls, every day. Virtual falls, be a better name. Watch the surface I'm walking on. Is it grass, as on a lawn? OK, not a bad place to fall. Is it sidewalk? Interior floor? Rug? Carpet? Tile? If it's bare earth, is it smooth? Rocky? Slanted? Whatever the surface, imagine falling on it, how it might feel. Be prepared. Try to go down in a sort of roll, instead of flat. Try to keep your head up. Avoid falling backward. That's a bad direction.

30 MAY

The 30th of May. My big day. Ninety-nine years ago I began my life in Stephenville Texas.

The time is now 3:30 p.m. and I have enjoyed a fine 99th birthday party, held here at the Winedale place. We had a houseful of guests.

Mark and Becky were here from Houston. I almost never get to see them both at the same time. And my grandchildren came,

Kacy from Houston and Daniel all the way from Alabama and Travis from Kansas. Also Will Warren and his wife Maren and their two kids, Declan and Maddie, all from New York City. And hey, even Maren's parents, Donna and Barry, were here from Buffalo, N.Y. *Buffalo!*

A splendid attendance, with everybody looking healthy and beautiful and intelligent and prosperous.

This was all Babette's idea and she was in charge. She served birthday cupcakes decorated with multiflavored ice cream. Original art by the Warren children was presented to the honoree (that's me). And Happy Birthday to Papa Hale was rendered by the attendees, in four different keys.

I am obliged to explain that all those guests were not present, physically, in our house. They attended my party via the electronic magic of Zoom. But for me, they were surely here, and they will never go away.

Winedale Publishing is a small Texas press,
founded in 1996, that publishes literary fiction and
creative nonfiction, including memoir. Our current interest is in
publishing regional titles of high quality that commercial
publishers routinely overlook.

We love stories and believe they are found everywhere.

_____

Our latest, and others by Leon Hale:

A WALL OF BRIGHT DEAD FEATHERS
by Babette Fraser Hale

"A vivid set of tales about connection to other people and to the
natural world…Hale's lovely prose show a keen eye for
detail, (as she) explores various women's familial and
romantic relationships."—*Kirkus Reviews*

ONE MAN'S CHRISTMAS
by Leon Hale

Holiday memories

OLD FRIENDS
by Leon Hale

His most recent column collection

SUPPER TIME
by Leon Hale

Food and recollections from a long life

BONNEY'S PLACE
by Leon Hale
His beer joint novel—warm and funny

ADDISON
by Leon Hale
A soldier in love, far from home

TURN SOUTH AT THE SECOND BRIDGE
by Leon Hale
Tales of extraordinary Texas characters

——

These and other books from Winedale Publishing may
be purchased through the Texas Book Consortium
(www.tamupress.com/consortium/winedale-publishing)

And from your favorite bookstore

For further information: www.winedalebooks.com